Awestruck

Awestruck

Life-Changing Encounters With Jesus

TIM COOPER

RESOURCE *Publications* • Eugene, Oregon

AWESTRUCK
Life-Changing Encounters With Jesus

Scripture taken from the HOLY BIBLE, NEW INTERNATIONAL
VERSION®. NIV®. Copyright © 1973, 1978, 1984. Used by permission of
Zondervan. All rights reserved.

Resource Publications
An Imprint of Wipf and Stock Publishers
199 W. 8th Ave., Suite 3
Eugene, OR 97401

www.wipfandstock.com

ISBN 13: 978-1-61097-090-7
Manufactured in the U.S.A.

To April, Makayla, Trace, and Lilly Grace
as we continue to love Jesus together.

"The beginning of the gospel about Jesus Christ, the Son of God."

—Mark 1:1

Contents

Acknowledgments

I'VE BEEN blessed with wonderful people in my life. There is not enough space to begin to tell the stories of inspiration around me. For each story I tell, I'm eternally blessed to know each friend within the context of their greater story.

April, I could never have dreamed of a better wife, mother to our children, or best friend. You possess a faith in Jesus that I aspire to attain. I love our journey together more with each new day.

The Momentum Christian Church family, I'm so excited to be on this journey with you as we grow together in the years to come.

The churches I've had the pleasure of serving, thanks for loving me and forming friendships that will last an eternity.

Preface

Have you ever met someone who changed your life? I carefully weaved my way in and out of traffic lanes managing to skillfully advance myself through the Friday afternoon rush hour traffic. There was no way I would be late to dinner. I was meeting the staff of the church where I would begin employment the next week and didn't want to portray myself in any way other than prompt, courteous, and professional. I arrived with one minute to spare.

I stood in the lobby introducing myself and learning about my new co-workers. They circled around me as if I was the new kid in a third-grade classroom. As I came to the end of the circle the Children's Minister caught my eye. Well, if I'm being honest, she actually caught my eye and took my breath before I made it all the way around the circle.

"Hi! I'm April," she bubbled over into my heart. We shared dinner that evening with a nightcap at the bowling alley. While everyone else on staff was present, there was only one presence of which I was concerned at that moment. The next few weeks found me trying to spend as much time as possible getting to know April.

April and I have been married for several years now. Through marriage, parenting, and everyday life she still takes my breath. I can honestly say she is the best thing about me. I can also honestly say that the encounter that Friday afternoon in the restaurant lobby completely changed my life forever.

Have you ever met someone who changed your life? Have you ever met someone who left you speechless? Have you ever met someone who left you amazed? Have you ever met someone who left you awestruck?

It was an everyday occurrence when real people encountered Jesus for the first time. Time after time they found their lives turned upside down after each encounter. There was the career fisherman who dropped his nets and found his cross. There was the crippled man taking his first steps. The blind opened their eyes to see Jesus for the first time. There was the woman who bled for more than a decade who rejoiced in her first day of relief. There was the father who welcomed his daughter back to life.

The Gospel of Mark captures these encounters and more. These weren't everyday encounters. These were life-altering events that changed the course of history one life at a time. Mark shows everyday men and women left awestruck by their encounters with God in the flesh finding new life and fresh perspective each step of the way. The best part is that God still desires those encounters for us today.

As I write this book, we are on an incredible journey of faith through an incredible vast unknown of our future. Several months ago, my wife and I decided to leave our ministry in a large church, with a large bank account and 80,000 square feet of facility space to lead a new church plant on the other end of town. God spoke in our lives and moved in ways that were undeniable. The journey has been full of God-moments where he rises up and inspires our faith in new ways as we prepare for the launch of Momentum Christian Church in 2011.

One of our initial challenges was in filling our staff positions with passionate and gifted individuals driven by the prospects of introducing new people to Jesus. We met Philip last Summer as we were beginning the process and knew he and his wife fit perfectly with the vision we were casting. The only problem is that Philip was employed by a stable church seven hours away surrounded by all of his family and his hometown which he held dear. Still, we felt God's leading to contact Philip.

Little did we know that Philip was encountering the call of Jesus at the same time through the faithful heart of his mother, Linda. Philip's father is in the military and was preparing at the time to be deployed to Afghanistan. Philip's two older brothers were also preparing to leave the hometown. Despite the upheaval faced by her family, Linda knew God was preparing Philip.

Just hours before I called Philip for the first time, Linda had a talk with her son. She told him that she felt God was preparing to call him to a ministry somewhere else and that he should not only listen, but he should follow that leading. She told him not to be worried about her and that she released him to follow God's calling. We were on the phone just a few hours later and Philip chose to join our team the next week.

As a parent, I've considered Linda's faith many times over the past few months. I've considered if I could let our children go. Even though our children are only twelve, ten, and three years-old, I've considered where God might be calling their lives for the first time. I've been inspired by Linda's faith to remember to encourage our children to follow that still-small voice.

None of what Linda did would have been possible without her life-altering relationship with Jesus. A relationship that encourages us to sacrifice in order to love more completely. A relationship that encourages us to persevere when we feel like giving up. A relationship with a Savior who pursues us passionately on a daily basis when we do everything in our powers to least deserve it.

Have you ever met someone who changed your life forever? Have you ever met Jesus? If this doesn't sound like the Jesus you know, this is your invitation to examine him through the perspective of some of his closest friends. This is your invitation to be awestruck through very real encounters when very real people encountered a very real Jesus.

1

Leaving Your Nets

"As Jesus walked beside the Sea of Galilee, he saw Simon (Peter) and his brother Andrew casting a net into the lake, for they were fishermen. 'Come, follow me,' Jesus said, 'and I will make you fishers of men.' At once they left their nets and followed him."

—Mark 1:16–18

WE ICED the drinks in the cooler, gathered our gear, and packed the car full of expectations for the day. It was to be a fishing day for the men. I was in 5th Grade and Grandpa was an expert fisherman. We were destined for success.

The skies began to darken a bit as we boarded the boat. The captain, a rusty veteran of the sea, seemed unfazed by the ominous clouds so I thought nothing of them either. I knew Grandpa was prepared for anything. We pushed off from the dock and soon found the Gulf coastline of southwest Florida vanishing from the horizon.

It didn't take long for crowds to gather around Grandpa. He fished with multiple hooks and often pulled multiple fish from the sea at the same time. I couldn't get a bite. He was catching sharks to thunderous applause.

The first clap of thunder in the distance was almost so faint that you couldn't distinguish the sound. It could have been someone moving a cooler around the deck or slamming a door on the other side of the boat. The second clap confirmed itself as the sky lit up in the distance. No more fishing.

Everyone huddled inside the boat's galley as we attempted to make our way back to shore. With each wave the seas became a bit larger. Grandpa, always prepared for anything, reached into his bag and offered up some medicine which he advised would help me to avoid becoming seasick. He explained that the medicine worked as a numbing agent to the stomach and prevented the stomach from becoming aggravated.

He also told me it was chewable.

It wasn't.

It didn't take long before I noticed my words beginning to slur. He asked me why I was chewing on my lip. I had no idea I was chewing on anything. My entire mouth, including my tongue and the insides of my cheeks, was completely numb. To make things worse, all of the numbing power of the medicine was applied to my mouth. That didn't seem to help my stomach.

We laughed about that day for a long time. The memory of that day and my fishing experience with my grandfather burns deep within me. Between the storm, seasickness, and a completely numb mouth, that day of fishing stands out as one I'll never forget. Peter had such a day on his boat once.

Peter and his brother Andrew were busy working the family business. They eagerly boarded the boat and cast out their nets each day, all the while hoping for something to happen. One day, something did happen. It left the brothers awestruck.

As the brothers prepared to cast their net for what must have felt like the hundredth time that day, Jesus called out from the shore, "Come, follow me and I will make you fishers of men." This encounter would lead Peter to a life of amazement and wonder following Jesus.

I would have been full of questions. Come where? Follow you where? Fishers of what? Am I going to need a bigger net?

Sometimes it's easy for questions to take the rudder when we encounter Jesus. Instead, Mark 1:18 says, "At once, they left their nets and followed [Jesus]." If you were judging reaction time, Peter and Andrew passed with flying colors. There was no hesitation, no questioning, no reservations. There was just an awestruck response. I would love for it to be said that I answer the call of God at once whenever he calls. Instead, I'm afraid, more often than not, I'm not so quick to drop the nets. How did Peter know? Where did his faith come from?

Is it any wonder that Peter quickly became a leader among the disciples and ultimately among the early Church? After all, Peter had the ability to make difficult decisions quickly. Where some would call Peter rash or impulsive, I would argue he was decisive. Did he make mistakes? You bet. I'm sure there were actions and statements he would have taken back in a heartbeat. Yet judging his life as a library of leadership decisions reveals that Peter, more often than not, chose a rash and impulsive faith if anything.

Peter's ability to make an instant decision to leave his nets brought about a life of abundant faith. I'm not so sure how I would have performed in that instant. Think it was easy? Peter chose to walk away from the family business which promised security, safety, and a solid path, for a life that he knew nothing about. I don't like the unknown. Odds are you don't either.

Back to the questions. Have you ever found it difficult to answer the call of God? Maybe you've asked questions. I know I have. "How do I know he's there?" "How do I know this is God's calling?" "Is this really what God would want me to do?" Rather than allowing our awestruck faith to take the rudder, we steer aimlessly back and forth hoping to run aground on God's calling.

Sometimes God calls us to step out on faith and not through impact. Sometimes God desires for us to step out rather than be pushed. Sometimes God desires for us to drop our nets rather than to hold on to our questions. Sometimes God calls us to get out of the boat and follow him when we can't even see the plan.

There was no way that Peter could have seen the plan for his life. There was no way he could have envisioned how his simple decision would change him and everyone around him forever. Some thought he was impulsive and rash that day. I think he was decisive in answering the call of God. That decision was truly life-changing.

It was a hot, dry, and dusty day that October as the people converged from the many roads that led to Rome. The celebration was to recognize Nero's tenth anniversary as Emperor of Rome. The year had been particularly difficult. The great fire of Rome caused a significant physical and economical strain on the center of the empire.

Each October the city erupted in a violent feast to celebrate the reigning emperor. The celebrations often featured the bloodshed of common criminals and sacrifices. The crowds would work themselves into drunken celebratory stupors. Not everyone, however, was celebrating that day in A.D. 64.

With each movement down the hall Peter knew that it could very well signal the arrival of his executioner. Peter had been warned about sharing the story of Jesus in Rome. He knew it could cost his life. Tradition holds that Peter even attempted to leave Rome but had another encounter with Jesus along the road which left him awestruck once again. He turned around and headed back into the famed city.

Peter knew his ending. He just didn't know when or where. His last encounter with Jesus featured another calling just like the first. John 21 records that following the resurrection Jesus spent a morning having breakfast with Peter by the shore. After a long discussion to affirm Peter's love and faith, Jesus said,

> "I tell you the truth, when you were younger you dressed yourself and went where you wanted; but when you are old you will stretch out your hands, and someone else will dress you and lead you where you do not want to go." Jesus said this to indicate the kind of death by which Peter would glorify God. Then he said to him, "Follow me!"

The executioner didn't lead Peter to the cross that morning. Peter followed Jesus there. It was there that tradition holds Peter made a request to be crucified upside down saying that he did not deserve to be crucified in the same manner as his Savior some three decades after leaving his nets by the sea. I wish I could have seen Peter's reunion with the Savior following his death. The nets suddenly seemed very insignificant.

They gathered for the celebration in the heat of the day. They worshipped through the sweaty afternoon to celebrate the 100th Anniversary of the first missionary arrivals in Zaire. The missionaries pushed towards the heart of the jungle which housed tribes with little to any knowledge of the outside world. The celebration rejoiced in the lives and deaths of many who dedicated themselves to sharing the news of Jesus in the remote area.

As the celebration neared the close a gray-haired man came forward from the back of the room insisting that he had something to share with the group or a vast secret would go to the grave with him. Those present shifted in their seats. After all, it was a hot day and the man was not on the program. What would he say? What would he do?

He began by recalling how the tribal leaders didn't know what to make of the Christian missionaries. The tribal leaders had little exposure to the outside world and no knowledge of Jesus. In order to judge the validity of the new message, the tribal leaders slowly began to poison the Christian missionaries. Gradually the first missionaries began to die from the poisoning.

The crowd had grown somber and began to process a mix of emotions as the old man became emotional in his story. The man began to smile. He said that the tribal leaders learned what a life with Jesus looked like through the deaths of his servants. They began to trust. They began to follow. They began to change. They were awestruck by how Jesus' followers died.

Peter taught that lesson all too well in the streets of Rome. The early Christians found peace, courage, and boldness through their leader who chose to loosen the clutch on the nets of life. Peter found out firsthand what it meant to be fishers of men.

What are you holding in your nets that keep you from following your God? Pride? Ambition? Fear? Selfishness? Control? It's so much easier for us to continue to cast our own nets rather than follow Jesus to something unknown. We avoid the unknown even when we know we don't like the known. We might dislike the unknown more. There might be pitfalls. There might be failure.

Corrie Ten Boom was a Dutch Christian who experienced the worst of the Holocaust of World War II. The Holocaust resulted in the deaths of more than six million Jews during that time. She did her best throughout the war to hide Jews being sought by the Nazi party. Eventually she was arrested and endured the hardships of the concentration camps alongside those she had worked so hard to protect. I saw an interview recorded nearly three decades later. When asked if she ever feared for her life, Corrie Ten Boom said, "Never be afraid to trust an unknown future to a known God."

Following Jesus means journeying deep into the adventurous unknown of our faith. Following Jesus means leaving our pride, ambition, and selfishness behind in the nets. Following Jesus means encountering pitfalls, snares, and traps. Following Jesus only occurs when we are awestruck by him. Following Jesus means dropping our nets.

It would have been easier for Peter to stay in the boat with his nets. It was the life he knew. Yet Peter responded to the adventurous journey of an awestruck faith. Jesus is asking you to follow him in the same way. Will you?

2

A New Teacher

*"They went to Capernaum, and when the Sabbath came, Jesus
went into the synagogue and began to teach."*

—Mark 1:21

I slowly made my way down the hall towards the bulletin board
that held the keys to my future. The trek normally wasn't as important as it was that particular day. The first day of school was approaching and it was time to find out who my new teacher would
be for the entire fifth grade year. There was one teacher's list where
I did not want to see my name listed.

She was six feet three inches tall and often walked around
school without her wig. She was rumored among the student
population to eat chalk, scream, and throw erasers and students.
She was rumored among the parents to be one of the best prepara-
tory teachers in the entire school. For students she was the end of
the world.

As I eased my way down the hallway I prayed like never before. It's amazing how faithful we become in times of panic. I also
began to make preparations in case my name appeared on the list.
I didn't have a lot of possessions as a fifth grade kid but I needed
to know where my GI Joes were going in case my world truly was
coming to an end.

There it was. My name was on the list of which I hoped it never would be. Thoughts immediately entered my head. What was my sister Becky going to do with 300 GI Joes, parts, and accessories? Would I at least get to finish my basketball season? Was this some sort of hidden camera show?

As an adult I look back on that year with great fondness now. It was one of my favorite years of school. She was one of my favorite teachers ever. I never saw her eat chalk or throw students. She did throw erasers but what's school without a little entertainment? Her methods and passion for teaching were unlike any other teacher I ever experienced.

Jesus' approach to teaching left many crowds awestruck. He was unlike any teacher they had ever heard before or would ever hear again. Jesus was different. Mark 2:21-28 records one of his earliest teaching moments on the Sabbath in Peter's hometown of Capernaum.

It didn't take long for the people to be awestruck by the teaching of Jesus. He entered the Synagogue that day and began to teach. Mark 2:22 says, "The people were amazed at his teaching, because he taught them as one who had authority, not as the teachers of the law." The people were amazed.

Teaching time was nothing new during a trip to the Sabbath. Each week the people gathered to hear one of the teachers of the law. The teacher would typically open and read from a commentary of the law written by other teachers. This particular week, the Son of God provided the commentary to the point that it amazed everyone who heard it because of the authority of his teaching. After all, he didn't have any unanswered questions. He was God in the flesh. It must have been amazing to hear The Word teach the word. But the experience didn't stop there for the members of the Capernaum synagogue.

Immediately a man in the synagogue who was possessed by an evil spirit began to cry out to Jesus in Mark 2:24, saying, "What do you want with us, Jesus of Nazareth? Have you come to destroy us? I know who you are—the Holy One of God!"

Nothing like that ever happens at my church. Imagine the kid complaining all the way to synagogue that morning because he didn't want to go to another boring meeting. He was interested now. Maybe we've come to expect the mundane because that's all the room we've allowed God in which to move.

Jesus called for the man to be silent and immediately ordered the evil spirit out of the man. Mark 2:26 says, "The evil spirit shook the man violently and came out of him with a shriek." It was a wild scene. Mark happened to have a great eye-witness of the account. Most scholars believe that Mark's Gospel is written as the first-person memories of Peter. After all, no one was closer to Jesus. Peter received an up-close and personal view of the scene in the synagogue.

The people were all so amazed by the scene in verse 27 that they asked, "What is this? A new teaching—and with authority! He even gives orders to evil spirits and they obey him." News of the day immediately spilled out of the synagogue into the whole region as soon as the doors opened.

Our world isn't big on authority. Culture has developed a relativistic flare in which it is no longer acceptable to tell anyone what is right or wrong or true or false. Jesus faced a similar cultural mindset in his time. First Century Palestine was an alphabet soup of philosophy. Jewish teaching divided between several competing schools of thought. The Romans brought their own mix of hedonism to the region. The Greeks in the region expounded the many philosophies being lectured in Athens. Our world isn't so different from the authority-starved environment in which Jesus ministered.

It was no coincidence that Jesus attended that Synagogue on that particular day with the possessed man. He was there for a reason. Jesus healed many during his ministry. His miracles stretched along the seashores, into the fields, and in the middle of the road. Yet, this particular healing occurred in the Synagogue.

Jesus could have met the demon-possessed man anywhere at anytime. He healed him in the Synagogue for three distinct reasons. First, it set his teaching apart from any other teacher the people had ever heard. After all, how many teachers of the law finished delivering their commentaries by healing a shrieking and wild demon-possessed man? None. Jesus revealed the true authority of his message through his power to heal.

The second unique message delivered through the healing in the Synagogue is that it began what would be a continuous pattern of Jesus performing miracles on the Sabbath. The Sabbath was the Jewish day of rest in which no work was to be performed. God presented the Sabbath to the people during the time of Moses as a day of rest to be kept holy.

The religious leaders developed thirty-nine man made areas in which work could not be done including carrying, cooking, stitching, piercing and more. There was even a limit to the amount of steps that could be walked. It became a symbol of the controlling religious establishment. The penalty for breaking the Sabbath was death according to several teachers of the law.

Jesus didn't choose to cook, walk a mile, or stitch a new robe that day. He chose to drive out a demon. It must have shocked the religious teachers. They couldn't find that one on their list anywhere. Time after time again Jesus would leave the crowds awestruck through Sabbath Day miracles only to anger the religious establishment who believed it better to allow individuals to continue to suffer for one more day rather than to make a difference on the Sabbath because it violated their tradition of piety.

The people recognized authority and they liked it. If they were being honest, they probably craved it. Week after week they attended the Synagogue to hear opinion. That day they heard authoritative truth. Despite our best lies we crave authority. The danger is what we do with it after we receive it.

I used to serve on staff at a downtown church. It presented challenges that went unseen to suburban churches. It also presented opportunities unique to our location and environment. We hosted a Day Camp one year in conjunction with a local inner city ministry and I learned a little about authority.

My wife and I volunteered to work with the preschool group for a day. I don't know if you've ever spent three and a half hours with preschool kids but you should whenever you get the chance. If nothing else, it gave me a whole new appreciation of the men and women who volunteer to work with our kids on a weekly basis. My wife is on the professional level as she spent ten tremendous years turning hearts to God as a Children's Pastor.

We took the kids outside to play with sidewalk chalk. Many of them had never used or seen sidewalk chalk. There was one boy who seemed to stretch my patience at every turn. As soon as we hit the sidewalk he became very anxious. "How far can we go?" I'll be honest I hadn't really thought about it. My wife and the other educator with us drew a line on the concrete not to be crossed. I thought the line would solve the problem. I was wrong.

I watched as the boy continued to draw more lines. Each line he drew closed the acceptable area a little bit more. He then began to chastise anyone who would cross his line. He announced that everyone must stay within his lines even though he didn't have the authority to make that decision or proclamation. He was given a large area to enjoy. Instead, he spent his time attempting to limit his enjoyment along with the freedom of everyone else in the group.

It's easy to be hard on the religious leaders of Jesus' time. Are we so much different? If we're being honest with each other for a moment we would have to admit that we're pretty pious about our traditions as the Church. God blesses the church that can distinguish the difference between His design and their desires. We spend a lot of time arguing over our pious traditions and desires. God spends a lot of time shaking his head. The result is that we miss the opportunity to be awestruck by the One who we are supposed to be about.

There is one more subtle message delivered by Jesus that morning in the Synagogue. He came to bring completion. Not only can Jesus save our lives and change them but his most fervent desire is to complete them. We are incomplete without his presence.

The people gathered for years to hear the commentaries and teachings of the Law and the Prophets of old. Yet, Jesus revealed that day that he was the completion of each. He didn't come to strike down God's Law. He came to complete it.

Jesus wants to complete your life as well. He has the authority to bring completion far greater than any religious tradition or pious man made regulations. Jesus has the ability to release your life to experience the relationship with God you've always dreamed about.

Fifth grade was my favorite year of school. Despite my greatest fears I learned more that year than any other I ever experienced. I particularly enjoyed a weekly project. Each week we were assigned with writing, creating, and illustrating a new book. The more creative the book produced, the better the grade. I found a love for writing that I never would have discovered if my name hadn't been on that list as I stood with sweaty palms and a broken heart that day so long ago. Mrs. Watts had an incredible impact on my life because she was a different type of teacher.

I wonder what would have happened if Jesus offered an invitation at the end of his teaching like we do in our church. I think the aisles would have been filled. After all, they witnessed him drive a demon out of the guy on the third row. They had to realize that Jesus had the authority and ability to know their hearts as well.

The people left the Synagogue awestruck that day. Mark 1:28 says, "News about [Jesus] spread quickly over the whole region of Galilee!" They experienced more than the mundane that day at the Synagogue as Jesus revealed his authority. This different type of teacher left them awestruck.

3

Filled with Compassion

"Filled with compassion, Jesus reached out his hand and touched the man. 'I am willing,' Jesus said."

—Mark 1:41

MY SISTER Rebecca is a teacher. She happens to teach third grade at an elementary school in an extremely impoverished area of her city. The economic disparity of the area has also created social difficulties which combine to make the district one of the most challenging socio-economic districts in the city. In the last three years of teaching she has had very few students with traditional two-parent homes. Most of her students come from broken homes with difficult stories. Many of them never experience love in any way at home. They draw pictures of her and give them as a gift because she is the only adult in many of their young lives that cares whether they wake up each morning or not.

The first day of school is less than a week away as I write this chapter. I've noticed her doing something this year that I've never seen her do before. She's visited the home of every student in her class prior to the start of school. She shared her experiences with us the other night. She was moved to tears by several of the homes. She was filled with compassion for the students who will struggle through poverty and nourishment deficiency this school year.

One home visit didn't go so well. The parent became quit agitated during the visit and began to threaten Rebecca physically. The threats were taken so seriously that security was added to her classroom for the annual Parent-Teacher Open House. The incident left several people shaken up and concerned to say the least.

My sister is a great teacher. She was recently featured on county-wide training videos for her ability to communicate educational concepts in certain areas of learning to third-grade minds. Her grades in school were fantastic and her professional accomplishments have set her apart in her field at an early stage of her career.

I say all this to say that sometimes I wonder why she does it. I wonder why she stays at a challenging school with impossible test score goals. I wonder why she stays at a challenging school lacking the parental and community financial funding found in other districts. I wonder why she stays at a challenging school in which she faces physical threats of violence.

The answer is simple. She loves the kids. She loves the community. She has a great compassion for the pain that surrounds her on a daily basis in the hallways, restrooms, cafeteria, and classrooms of her school.

One of the beautiful things about having four different gospel narratives telling the story of Jesus is the ability for the authors to focus on distinct portraits of Jesus' personality. Mark chooses to spend a great deal of time discussing the compassion of Jesus and portraying Jesus with people in situations that we certainly would find less than appealing. Peter must have recalled the compassion of Jesus with such reverence as he told the story of Jesus to Mark. The Holy Spirit made sure that compassion was a character trait revealed so wonderfully in Mark's writing.

The first encounter with the compassion of Jesus comes in Mark 1:40-45 as Jesus encountered a leprous man. Leprosy was no joking matter. Lepers were typically the outcast of society. No one wanted the dreadful disease to spread into their lives. I can't blame them.

Leprosy facilitated the decay of the skin and body. While extremely uncommon today, it does still exist in third world countries lacking in medical advancements. Try looking up pictures online of leprosy and you'll quickly understand why the people of Jesus' day tried to keep them separated from the rest of society. An individual battling leprosy often loses their fingers, nose, ears, and any other affected areas.

Lepers were required by law in First Century Palestine to stay away from society. They lived in their own colonies far from the possibility of contacting healthy individuals. Lepers also carried bells to ring in case of coming near civilization so normal folks would know to hide themselves from the infected. Lepers were to announce themselves as "unclean."

Needless to say, lepers didn't have a lot of social interaction. Imagine a life of loneliness, listening to mothers scream at your very appearance while they shield their children. Imagine the physical pain of the disease. Imagine the emotional pain of watching your body fall apart before your very eyes. Imagine a life with no one to love, no one to give you a chance, no one to believe in you, no one to draw you close. It's easy to understand why lepers were considered cursed and some literally wished to die.

That's what makes the encounter with Jesus so special in Mark 1:40. Mark records that the man with leprosy approached Jesus, fell to his knees, and cried, "If you are willing, you can make me clean." What a prayer. It's probably slightly different from the prayers we pray. "God if you could find a way. . . ." "God if you could figure out . . ." Instead, this man who was broken by life and ignored by society said, "God, I know you can if it fits your will."

I love Mark 1:41. It's a reminder to me on a regular basis when my temperature begins to rise and my blood pressure begins to boil. It's a call to a deeper relationship and a deeper walk with my Savior. Mark 1:41 says, "Filled with compassion, Jesus reached out his hand and touched the man."

Did you catch that? The God of the Universe, the Creator of the sun, moon, planets, and stars, was filled with compassion for one of us and the beautiful part about it is Jesus wasn't just compassionate about him, he's compassionate about us as well. Think about that. Jesus is filled with compassion when he looks at us mired in our pain and brokenness. Jesus literally hurts when we hurt.

Jesus was also very intentional in how he dealt with the man. He didn't just speak a healing as he did in other parts of Scripture. Jesus reached out and touched the untouchable. Jesus loved the unloveable. Jesus reached for the same man others ran from.

There was a powerful statement about Jesus in a simple touch. "I am willing," Jesus said. "Be clean!" Immediately the leprosy left him and he was cured." The power of the moment, however, is not just the fact that the man was finally free of his dreadful disease. The power is that Jesus chose to heal him in a way to make sure that people knew he was different. Jesus presents to us a model of leadership not based on power but on compassion.

What if we began to live that way? What if our life's pursuits were not based as much on power as on compassion? What if we began to live out the compassion evident in not just the teaching but the acts of Jesus? What if our churches strived to be led by compassion instead of the pursuit of power? Our world would look so very different that I doubt we would even recognize what surrounded us.

Jesus warned the man not to tell anyone about the healing. That's like me telling you not to let anyone know you just found a million dollars in your basement. The passion and urgency of the man to tell the story was undeniable. Mark 1:45 says, "Instead he went out and began to talk freely, spreading the news. As a result Jesus could no longer enter a town openly but stayed outside in lonely places."

To put it simply, the man couldn't help but spread the news about Jesus. He was determined to bring fame to Jesus. What are you doing in your life to make Jesus famous to your friends, family, neighbors, or community? We probably let out a collective sigh because we know we're not doing enough.

Wait a minute. That guy was delivered from an evil disease. He was dying. He was hopeless. There was no way that guy could have saved himself. There was no way anybody else could have saved him either. He had a reason to make Jesus famous to those around him.

So do we. You see, this wasn't the last act of compassion from Jesus. The final act of his ministry included the ultimate act of compassion. He reached out once more, this time to be nailed to a crude wooden cross for you and for me. We were stricken with an evil disease called sin. No medicine or doctor could save us. Our freedom could only be brought about by an act of compassion from the God of the Universe. We have a reason to make Jesus famous.

On October 25, 2010, a tsunami struck the Indonesian Islands following a large underwater earthquake killing hundreds on the islands. The tragedy of the event is that it didn't have to happen. Following the massive Tsunami which killed nearly 300,000 residents of the Pacific rim islands in 2004, scientists installed DART buoys in the waters surrounding the islands. The buoys are designed to alert scientists and early detection alarms of large waves approaching the shore. The DART buoys, however, failed to work on October 25, 2010, and hundreds were killed as a result.

We're a lot like those buoys. In a world that is dark and cold, we are the last line of warning to those in danger. If we remain silent, what will happen to those we love?

What will happen to our neighbors?

What will happen to our friends?

What will happen to our families?

It's time that we possess a sense of urgency to make Jesus famous in this world.

4

An Authentic Moment

"But that you may know that the Son of Man has authority on earth to forgive sins . . ."

—Mark 2:10

THE SUN is glaring at me this morning through the sliding glass doors to the balcony as I sit in the condo and write overlooking the Atlantic Ocean. We've made our annual trek to the beach with our extended family on my wife's side. It's been quiet to write this morning but everyone is beginning to stir. There are eleven of us in the condo. Three of those are under the age of three. I might have to get up earlier in the morning.

Yesterday we played for a long time on the beach. I laid out with my wife, April, played football with my ten year-old son, Trace, jumped big waves with my twelve year-old daughter, Makayla, and played in the sand with my three year-old, Lilly. It was one of those days that leave you absolutely drained from the intense rays of sunshine and exhaustive pounding of the surf yet you can't wait to do it all again the next day. I might need a vacation from my vacation to get rested up.

Lilly has an affinity for sea shells. Our condo is one of those beach-decorated places featuring coral colors and fake sea shells in each room. They just don't seem to hold the same favor with her. Yesterday as I picked up a new book I've wanted to read for several months I heard Lilly shriek with excitement. "These real sea-sails," she screamed in her best southern drawl as she ran towards our tent with her net in hand. "Real sea-sails!"

We like things to be real. We crave authenticity. We're not big on fakes. This coming from a society which has successfully created, developed, and marketed such substitutions as margarine, salt substitutes, laminate wood floors, and social interaction through the screen of a phone or computer.

Despite our creativity for substitutions, we really crave authenticity. Don't believe me? We only use those substitutions because we can't afford the real products. We can't afford the caloric count of butter so we choose margarine instead. We can't afford the sodium count of table salt so we choose a flavorful substitute. We can't afford the cost of true hard-wood so we choose the laminate floor and lay it carefully under the watchful eyes of our wives (maybe that's just me). We can't afford the time for conversation but we can send a message of 140 characters or less to 552 friends in less than thirty seconds. We don't choose substitutes because we like them better. We choose them because they are more convenient or they cost less.

My mom went to a purse party not to long ago. I never knew they had purse parties. She was overwhelmed. They had every type of expensive purse that women want at a fraction of the retail price. Some of the purses were even considered deep discounts at as much as 80 percent off the retail price. Even though she thought that sounded like fun she thought something must be a little fishy. She didn't buy a purse that night. The purse party guy was arrested a few weeks later for selling fraudulent purses. All of the sudden there was no value in the discounted price because they weren't real.

I was watching one of the morning news shoes not to long ago and they were chronicling the rise of online dating. People don't even have time to build romantic connections face to face. Another unique angle is speed-dating. Guests spend five minutes with each other until the bell rings. Once the bell rings the date rotates to the next guest. After all, it would take months to go out with that many people to find the right mate.

We have masterfully created the artificial, designed the synthetic, and rejoiced in our own substitutions. We've created convenience around every corner. The problem is that our conveniences have left us starving for something real, craving something authentic. We are searching for something real like never before.

The marketing industry knows that quite well. Why else would a cola espouse itself as the real thing? Do you really think a generic cola could possibly taste better than the real one? The word 'real' is pretty hot. I just googled the word and got 3,960,000,000 responses in 0.12 seconds. When Google gives you nearly four billion results in a tenth of a second you know someone is searching for something.

Another result of our world of artificial replacements is that we don't easily identify what is real and what is not. And so we approach the thought of following Jesus with our standardized questions. How do we know he is genuine? Couldn't we just use another substitute? How do we know this is real and therefore better than the countless other options on the shelf that might not cost as much?

It's not the first time he's faced those questions. Jesus lived in a similar culture. He wasn't the only man claiming to be the Messiah in First Century Palestine. The Jews had long awaited their Savior. A new man arose each week it seemed to claim to be the Messiah sent to lead a revolt against Rome and free the Jews. We don't remember their names. We don't have followings named after them 2,000 years later. Their followers didn't continue to die after they themselves were martyred. Their movements didn't continue to move because nobody wants to follow a fake.

The religious establishment didn't know what to make of Jesus. There was no way to deny he cast out demons and healed leprosy. But was that enough to anoint him? Maybe he was just a common magician hypnotically altering the crowds. Maybe there was nothing wrong with the people in the first place. They didn't know what to make of Jesus. So, they decided to examine the product a little closer.

Mark 2:1 says that Jesus again entered Capernaum. I love the next phrase. Mark says, "The people heard that he had come home." You can translate that as "the people knew he was back to put on a show for them." Capernaum was surely burning with discussions about the rumors of the wonders Jesus performed in the countryside. Now, the people thought, surely he's going to do some of that here.

Some believe that the gathering actually took place in the home of Peter. So many people arrived to explore Jesus that a problem quickly arose. Mark 2:2 says, "So many gathered that there was no room left, not even outside the door, and he preached the word to them." The house was full and completely surrounded.

I think Jesus had a sense of humor. He knew the people were there to see more miracles. The crowds had heard by this time about the healings and exorcisms. Most of the crowd probably witnessed the exorcism of the demon-possessed man in the synagogue some time earlier. They were ready for more. Mark carefully records that Jesus preached the word to them. He didn't start the day with miracles or wondrous signs like they had come to see. He taught. The crowds continued to swell as the words of the prophet were unlike any they had ever heard before.

This presented a definite problem to one group of men attempting to reach Jesus. They were carrying their paralytic friend to Jesus. They knew Jesus was the real thing. If they could just get their friend to him they knew he would be healed.

Other men might have turned around when they saw the crowds. We're not sacrificial by nature. Still, this man's friends pressed on undaunted by the fact they couldn't get in the front door. They were determined to place their friend at the feet of Jesus.

First Century homes were basic one to two room buildings with a baked thatch-like roof. Most homes featured a set of steps of the side of the building so one could work on his roof with ease. The men ascended the rooftop with their friend and began to dig. You can see where this is going.

I love this narrative because I can see lots of guys I know. I live in the south. Southern men aren't deterred by obstacles. We fix them with duct tape, scraps of rope, and a whole lot of personality. Mark 2:4 says the men "made an opening in the roof above Jesus and after digging through it, lowered the mat the paralytic man was lying on." Can't get through the front door? No problem we'll come through the roof. It was a sort of First Century pit crew.

I wonder what the homeowner thought. I'd like to envision that he was sitting close to Jesus. After all, if you're hosting the crowd in your home you probably saved your seat pretty close to the front. He began to feel some dust falling on his head. Sometimes bringing people to Jesus gets messy. We're tempted to simply sit at his feet. Sometimes we're even annoyed when we're pushed outside of that comfort zone. He turned to look-up and saw a man on a mat coming through his roof. Does insurance cover that? Who's going to fix that?

It didn't surprise Jesus. He's God after all. He knew they were coming. He could see them walking down the street, frustrated by the crowd, hatching their scheme, climbing the steps, and digging through the thatch. He saw one more thing as well. Mark 2:5 says, "Jesus saw their faith." What a thought. What would it be like if Jesus saw our faith? The scary thing is that I know he sees my lack of faith as well.

I wonder if the guys on the roof high-fived, fist-bumped, or had that we-knew-it-all-along grin to each other. Now it was up to Jesus. They leaned in towards the opening in the roof as their buddy flashed a thumbs-up from the floor of the home and grinned at Jesus. He was ready to walk. He had no doubt Jesus could heal him.

Jesus saw their faith, examined their hearts, looked around the room and said, "Son, your sins are forgiven." Huh? They wondered if Jesus was confused for a minute. After all, they weren't here about their sins. The guy on the mat said something like, "Thanks, but . . ." Or maybe he was just silent from his confusion. The rest of the crowd was confused as well. This was the point where Jesus healed people, not talked about sins.

There was one group in the crowd not confused. The teachers of the law were furious, thinking to themselves, "Why does this fellow talk like that? He's blaspheming! Who can forgive sins but God alone?" (Mark 2:7). Essentially, does this guy really think he's God? Does he really think he's the Messiah?

Remember how Jesus could see the guys walking down the street, climbing the steps, and digging on the roof? He could see inside the hearts of the teachers of the law as well. Jesus immediately asked them, "Why are you thinking these things?" It's interesting to watch facial expressions when emotions turn from smug self-righteousness to absolute fear. That's what everyone in the room watched on the faces of the teachers of the law.

In Mark 2:9 Jesus says, "Which is easier: to say to the paralytic, 'Your sins are forgiven,' or to say, 'Get up, take your mat and walk?'" I would have asked if that was a trick question. They both seem pretty difficult to me. For the religious teachers, however, Jesus knew their answer would be that it would be more difficult to forgive sins because, after all, only God can do that. Jesus answered their silence once again, "That you may know that the Son of Man has authority on earth to forgive sins…I tell you, get up, take your mat and go home."

I love the next verse. Mark 2:12 says, "He got up, took his mat and walked out in full view of them all." I think he stared at the religious establishment on the way out the door. Everyone was left awestruck and an impromptu time of worship erupted in the home. The homeowner didn't care so much about his roof anymore.

That day was much more than just a paralytic walking for the first time. It would have been amazing if it stopped there. That day was about establishing Jesus as the genuine article. Jesus showed there was a greater purpose in his miracles than just the physical healing. His miracles validated his identity as the genuine Son of God. No imitations accepted. No substitutions needed.

I wonder sometimes if Jesus isn't trying to deliver the same message to us. I have a friend who struggles with his faith. He really wants to believe. He just doesn't seem to be able to muster the faith necessary. He told me one time that if he could just witness the miracles of Jesus he would believe instantly, no questions asked. Maybe he would, but I doubt it. The Gospel narratives are filled with instances where people witnessed Jesus' miracles only to ask more questions or choose not to be changed by their brush with God in the flesh.

Jesus taught an important lesson that day in the home with a hole in the roof. As the crowds leaned in to witness the miracle, Jesus taught them that it was the message of eternity that mattered most. How many of us spend our lives searching for a miracle and ignoring the gift of eternity? The man could have left the home on the mat on which he arrived and would have been better off for eternity after having his sins forgiven.

You've probably never heard of Simon bar Kokhba. Many believed him to be the Messiah. He led a revolt against the Romans. It was the last revolt of the Jewish-Roman Wars. He had quite the following. His army enlisted 300,000 Jews and an additional 100,000 militia members of varying descent. He claimed to be the long-awaited Messiah and many believed and followed him resulting in 580,000 fatalities and an ever stronger hold on the region by the Roman Empire.

Jesus never had 300,000 followers to the best of my calculations. Yet his message, validated by miracles such as the one at the home in Capernaum that day so long ago, has stood the test of time. Followers of Jesus make up a third of the world's population and are the largest such following in the world, all because he was real. In a world constantly searching for authenticity, Jesus not only talked the talk but he walked the talk as well.

Our world isn't so different today. If we're honest, we're all searching for something real. Maybe it's real purpose, real love, a real relationship, real significance, or a real hope. We've worn tired of the imitations. We've grown weary of the improvisations. We desire authenticity. Try lowering your mat at Jesus' feet for a while.

5

The Calm during the Storm

"Jesus got up, rebuked the wind and said to the waves, 'Quiet! Be still!' Then the wind died down and it was completely calm."

—Mark 4:39

I GREW up in Orlando, Florida. Orlando is known for a couple of things. Walt Disney World and Lightning. You're probably more familiar with the claim to Walt Disney World. However, Central Florida is also the lightning capital of the world. An average afternoon thunderstorm in Orlando can feature as many as 4,000 radar-confirmed lightning strikes. I always found it troubling that we sold the entire world on the idea of visiting the Sunshine State, only to be greeted by daily lightning storms during the summer months of the year. The interesting part about daily storms in Central Florida is that they come out of nowhere and often don't last very long.

Another interesting thing about living in Central Florida is that everyone wants to come visit you. I doubt people travel to visit their family and friends living in Bismark. A fourth-cousin in Orlando, however, reconnects long-lost families and reestablishes kindred friendships. Our house growing up was often a revolving door of friends and family. I loved it. It was an opportunity to spend priceless time with family and friends while actually having an excuse to do the regular tourist thing as well.

We were particularly excited one year when, literally, everyone related to my dad came to stay for a few days. There was an old lighthouse on the coast that offered daily tours and stood as a testament to some sort of oceanic history that we had long desired to tour. The extended family loaded up in what seemed like a ten car motorcade and departed for the sunny Florida coastline.

I'll admit it was a little cloudy when we arrived at the lighthouse but I wasn't the one making the decisions. After all, when you have a ten car motorcade of extended family members decision making becomes more of a mob mentality. Everyone is brave in a mob so we decided to press on with our lighthouse tours despite the distant rumble of thunder. Bad idea. Very bad idea.

It didn't take long to realize we were the only ones in the old lighthouse. That's usually an ominous sign in horror movies. I've found it translates to real life as well. We ascended the steps which spiraled around the center core of the structure. As we reached the top of the lighthouse and entered the observation deck I noted the wire cage and metal roof encasing us.

We all noticed the massive storm quickly pushing towards the lighthouse. Once again the mob mentality pushed forward, because in a mob, everyone feels safe. That feeling began to erode very quickly. The rain began to pelt the metal roof of the lighthouse as it penetrated the wire walls of safety. We all moved into the core of the lighthouse onto the steps to ensure a dry location. What happened next is somewhat of a blur.

Some family members believe an area near the lighthouse was struck by lightning. Others of us believe the lighthouse itself was struck. Flames began shooting from the electrical wiring of the historic structure all around us. The emotion of the mob quickly turned from safety to sheer panic.

Family members of advanced age began to sprint down the stairs and out of the lighthouse only to end up prostrate in the puddle of mud outside the front entrance. Voices were raised. Children were deserted, spouses were separated, memories were repressed, and stories were formed that will last a lifetime. For some reason in life, we remember the storms.

I have to believe that Peter remembered the storm quite well. Jesus' young ministry had already attracted a large following. He was teaching and healing at every turn. Jesus needed a break. In Mark 4:35, Jesus turned to his disciples and proposed they take a boat to the other side of the lake for a time of rest.

Mark 4:37 says "a furious squall came up, and the waves broke over the boat, so that it was nearly swamped." There are a couple of things we know about this account. First, it's being recalled by a rough and tumble fisherman, a guy who spent his life on the water. Second, this man of the sea was terrified along with his fellow fishermen. The storm was so ferocious that the waves broke over the boat.

Most of the time, we look for the calm before the storm. Sometimes we anticipate the calm after the storm. But if we really look intently to Jesus, we might just find the calm during the storm. That's what the disciples discovered that day on the boat and it left them awestruck.

Amidst their fear the disciples turned to Jesus that day on the water. Mark is intentional in revealing the fact that Jesus was sleeping in the stern of the boat. How could he sleep at such a time? How could he sleep through such a storm? When you knitted creation into existence a little wind and water doesn't bother you.

Mark 8:38 says, "The disciples woke [Jesus] and said to him, 'Teacher, don't you care if we drown?'" I think Mark is probably entirely too kind to the disciples. The scene was probably much more like this: "The disciples *shook* Jesus and *screamed* at him, 'Teacher, don't you care if we drown?'" I don't know about you, but I find myself screaming at God a lot during the storms of life. It's our natural response. We kick. We scream. We shake with fear.

The disciples knew that fear first hand that day on the sea. The Sea of Galilee was surrounded by mountains which frequently hid the ominous storms from the horizon. Matthew 8 says the storm emerged "without warning." The disciples had no time to prepare for the storm. Their plans weren't made. Their emergency plans weren't written.

That's when storms hit us—when we least expect it. Maybe you've been met with the unexpected illness, surprising loss of a job, or financial ruin that never seemed to be on the horizon. Maybe your marriage evaporated before you even knew it was in trouble. Odds are, when the storm hit, you didn't expect it.

One of my wife's friends stopped her a few months ago. April could tell there was something wrong but had no idea the entirety of the story about to emerge. Her friend began to tell her about the weekend she had experienced. Her family spent an amazing day together on Saturday. They attended church together Sunday morning and enjoyed a great lunch. The kids went to play with some friends and so they enjoyed each other as a couple all afternoon on Sunday. It was while laying in bed on what seemed to be the perfect Sunday afternoon that her husband turned to her, confessed an affair, announced he was moving in with the other woman that evening, and told her he wanted a divorce. She was in the storm. The waves were topping the boat. She never saw it coming.

One thing about growing up with Florida storms was also experiencing hurricane seasons. There were plenty of false alarms when everyone's 3-D Viper, Triple Doppler, scientific radar failed to accurately project the path of the storm. There were also some direct hits. I remember staying awake all night in college on the campus of my small Bible College as a freshman and watching the hurricane deposit two feet of water and bend palm trees parallel to the ground. I also remember working to board the windows and fill sandbags in anticipation of the storm.

When we know the storm is coming we have time to prepare for it. It doesn't seem to shock us as badly. The disciples were shocked. What seemed like an easy trip across the lake had now turned into a struggle for life or death.

I wonder what they did after they screamed at Jesus. Were they working on bailing the water? Were they trying to hold the rudder firm? I wonder if they just stood their in utter awe because they knew deep down after all that they had seen from this son of the carpenter that somehow he could make it all go away.

I love the response of Jesus. Mark 4:39 says, "He got up, rebuked the wind and said to the waves, "Quiet! Be still!" I wonder sometimes how he said it. Did he scream with a booming voice revealing the power residing in him as the creator? Or did he whisper with that still small voice that has spoken to so many through the years? I don't know but I like to think he whispered. I like to picture Jesus amidst the noise and violence of the storm whispering it into extinction. Mark says the winds died down and it was "completely calm." There wasn't even a hint of a white cap. No sign of the violent wind.

I believe that Jesus rebuked the storm with a whisper that day for a reason. You see, when we live a life with him, there is calm during the storm. He's not a frantic God who has lost control of his creation as some would argue. He's not a God who has placed his creation in place and walked away. My God speaks to the wind and the waves because he cares for us even during the storm.

After calming the wind and the waves, Jesus turned to address his followers. "Why are you so afraid? Do you still have no faith?" I would love to have been the proverbial fly on the wall of the boat at that moment. Have you ever seen the look on a child's face when their parents ask them "What were you thinking?" or "What were you trying to do?" It's that look that says, there's nothing good I can say right now.

A lot of times we get caught up believing that faith in the New Testament was easy. If I could only see Jesus then I would believe. If I could have only witnessed Jesus' miracles then I would follow faithfully. If I could just see the storm calmed then I would follow him without reservation or doubt. Really? Would we? I doubt it.

Despite all that the disciples had seen from Jesus to this point in his ministry, they still feared the storm. Despite witnessing him calm the storm they still doubted him. One denied him three times. One even betrayed him. My point is that seeing isn't always as easy as believing because the waves are still big, the wind still blows hard, and our fears are still real.

The event did stir them into a faith discussion amongst themselves. Mark 4:41 says, "They were terrified and asked each other, 'Who is this? Even the wind and the waves obey him!'" I don't think they were asking the question as if they didn't know. It's more rhetorical in nature as if to say, "We've never seen anyone like him before."

These seasoned fishermen had seen many storms come and go. They spent much of life witnessing the effects of such storms and learning to fear the storm. In one instant, in one moment, Jesus showed he commands the storm. They were awestruck. There's no reason to fear the storm, after all, there is a calm during the storm. His name is Jesus.

6

Love at All Costs

"So the man went away and began to tell the Decapolis how much Jesus had done for him. And all the people were amazed."

—Mark 5:20

I DIDN'T realize he was yelling at me. I should have. There was no one else pumping gas at ten o'clock at night. He continued to scream and walk towards me. It was obvious he had had a few too many drinks that night. I had no idea what my inebriated new friend was screaming about but it was clear he was angry at me.

As he moved closer I began to piece together a few words as he stumbled and slurred. "You pumpin' my gas." I was pretty sure he didn't own the gas station and even if he had I had prepaid for my gas so I was even more confused. He then began to slur other words that I can't put in writing here.

It also became clear that he was intent on settling this gas-pumpin' issue man to man. He envisioned old fashioned fisticuffs. I envisioned front page headlines of a pastor beating a drunk in a gas station parking lot. That's the stuff that sells small town newspapers. At least I think it does.

He slowly cocked his arm back with his hand formed into a fist and stumbled into punching motion. I would like to say at this point that I diffused the situation with some sort of powerful physical response. I wouldn't even mind telling you I talked the guy out of his punch with my massive counseling ability. I didn't really do anything amazing. As the punch awkwardly approached me, I simply side-stepped, stuck out my foot, and watched the man trip and fall to the ground while hitting his head against the gas pump.

The man was motionless for a few seconds. That was long enough for the newspaper headlines to emerge. "Pastor beats drunk." "Pastor slams drunk against gas pump." Even worse, I saw a movie one time where a guy punched a guy out of self-defense and killed the guy. He went to prison for life. I was considering what high-priced local attorney could free me or at least reduce my charge. Should I plea? Would I look good in stripes or do they wear orange now? Do pastors get private cells?

As I considered my future incarceration the gas station attendants reached the pump as the man began to come to. He looked up and began to cry. One of the worst things you can ever do in life is make a drunk cry. He sobbed heavily as he began to apologize for his actions. Apparently he was supposed to get gas on the way home for his wife's truck but had forgotten. When he pulled in and saw me pumping gas he knew there wouldn't be any gas left. Alcohol doesn't always render the most rational of thought processes.

The gas station employees said they were going to call the cops. He quickly dried his tears, got back into his truck, and drove off into the dark night. I didn't quite know how to tell my story when I got home but I knew I had a good one. As good as my story chronicling a confrontation with a crazed man was it wasn't as good as the story of the disciples from Mark 5. Shortly after watching Jesus calm the raging seas, the disciples witnessed Jesus healing a raging man as they left their boat on the lakeshore.

They saw him for the first time as they stepped out of the boat. He was known in the community as being possessed by an evil spirit. Not exactly the kind of guy you want for a next door neighbor. He had lived in the tombs outside of town and had grown so powerful with the evil spirits that no one in town could bind him or chain him. Every time someone tried to chain him, he broke the chains and terrorized all around him.

He was, in effect, a raging beast who haunted the burial tombs outside of town. At night, Mark tells us, the man would sit in the tombs cutting himself with sharp stones and filling the night sky with the sound of his cries. To make the man even more intimidating, Luke reveals the man was naked. Not exactly the welcoming party you expect to greet a king making landfall.

Jesus, however, was a different type of King. He didn't encounter the demon-possessed man by happenstance. Instead, Jesus encountered the man all society would turn from on purpose. Jesus actually sought out the naked, raging, possessed, beast that made the rest of society shutter. I can't help but admit that makes me a little uncomfortable.

I like the people in the city. You know, the ones who love their families, work hard, pay their taxes, live by the rules, practice good hygiene, drive nice cars, listen to my music, watch my television shows, cheer for my teams, and generally look like me. Jesus made it his point to love the rest of society—the ones we label unlovable.

Maybe that's why Mark spends so much time on this encounter. This isn't the first exorcism to be recorded by Mark (1:21–28; 1:32–34; 3:11–12). It also isn't the last. Yet this encounter gets an in depth treatment not found in the other encounters. Any author will tell you that word counts reveal a great deal about their priorities in writing. Mark devotes twice the amount of words to the encounter than does Matthew. I'm convinced that Mark spent so much time weaving this story because his intent was to show what happens when we are truly awestruck by the power and nature of Jesus. What better way to illustrate that point than to paint the context of this man of whom we certainly would have called the police if he attended one of our worship gatherings?

Jesus did not shy from the poor, the hurting, the afflicted, the dirty, or even the demon possessed. Instead, Jesus revealed one of his greatest characteristics—compassion. We like to picture Jesus certain ways. There's the infant Jesus, the wise Jesus, the powerful Jesus, the miraculous Jesus. How many of us instantly picture the compassionate Jesus? Is there any greater attribute of his character?

I can't help but be overwhelmed by that thought this morning. I'm writing from my dining room table and looking at our Christmas tree. It's Christmas Eve and for a rare occasion there is snow on the ground at Christmas here in Kentucky. Our lights are lit, presents are wrapped, and our agendas are filled. The sights, sounds, and smells of Christmas permeate the atmosphere around our every move. Yet I find myself convicted this morning for two reasons.

On one hand, my heart is broken for the 25,000 children who will die from starvation and preventable diseases around our world today. That number of deaths grows a little larger each day. That's one of the reasons why Christmas is a little different for our family this year. We'll still celebrate together but we will be solemnly aware of the crisis of starving and diseased orphans worldwide.

Have you ever had a moment that changed your life? We have. It actually started with a moment that broke our hearts. To understand our journey to where we are this Christmas, you have to understand where it started.

Last year was an amazing year for our family. Our daughter, Makayla, excelled on the Varsity Middle School Volleyball team and made first chair flute in the concert band. Our son, Trace, experienced great success with his All-Star baseball team which finished 5th place in the Ohio Valley Region of Cal Ripken baseball out of hundreds of teams from thousands of leagues. Both Makayla and Trace excelled in school academically. Our three-year old, Lilly Grace, developed her gift of conversation and had the opportunity to visit Cinderella in her castle at Walt Disney World for her third birthday party.

With little to no running experience prior to last year, my wife, April, ran nearly 1000 miles and completed multiple races with competitive times, including two half-marathons within a month of each other. She also continued with her substitute teaching. Most importantly, she invested in the development of our children every single day.

Aside from family achievements, we had an amazing year professionally as well. My first book, *Miles Past Normal*, was published last year and the opportunities that presented themselves due to the book far exceeded our expectations. We both traveled to Baltimore, Maryland, in September to be assessed for a new direction in our lives and were affirmed to a calling God laid on our hearts to plant a new church in Lexington, Kentucky.

Amidst all of these wonderful things, God was doing something else in our hearts as well. We were challenged midway through the summer at a conference we attended to "allow God to disturb us and break our hearts." I was traveling and speaking about my book which encouraged readers to take miles past normal steps of faith and began to wonder what God had in store in that way for our family.

At the same time, April ran across the blog of one of her sorority sisters from college. What she saw moved her more than she even realized at that point. April's friend's family adopted a child from Ethiopia. She began to share the story with our entire family.

As our family learned of the poverty, disease, and hopeless life faced by 150 million orphans worldwide, we were also confronted with the calls of scripture for followers of Jesus to make a difference in the lives of those orphans. After nearly six months of prayer, research, soul-searching, more research, and more prayer, we have been approved to adopt a child from Ethiopia in order to provide hope for the hopeless.

We're on the waiting list to adopt a child from Ethiopia through a wonderful God-honoring international agency. I can't help but wonder what the new addition to our family is experiencing this Christmas Eve. My heart aches far past the questions of gender or age that await our family. Is our child hungry? Is our child lonely? Is our child scared?

That's when I'm reminded of the Christmas story. You see, God became a baby for all of us, including the hungry, the lonely, and the scared. My God walked this Earth to connect and restore real lives like the child we're waiting to meet, the pilot who lives across the street, the medical sales rep next door, and even a crazy, deranged, naked, demon-possessed man on the shore so long ago.

I wonder what the disciples' first instincts were as the crazed man approached. Peter probably reached for his sword. John probably tried to calm everybody down. Judas made sure he had the money secured. As he got closer, they had to be surprised at what the man was screaming, "What do you want with me, Jesus, Son of the Most High God?"

I think God has a sense of humor in how he helps us grow in our faith at times. The disciples had just experienced a powerful storm on the water in which they were sure they were going to die. After Jesus calmed the storm, the disciples turned to each other and asked, "Who is this? Even the winds and the waves obey him."

Apparently the crazed, naked, bleeding, demon-possessed man understood Jesus' identity. At least, the demon inside of him did. The demon continued, "Swear to God that you won't torture me!" This part of the narrative disturbs me on a deep level. You see, it's not just enough to believe. The demon that day believed Jesus was God.

Jesus entered into a conversation with the demon, "What is your name?" By the time the greetings were exchanged it was revealed that the demon's name was Legion and that there were actually many demons possessing the man. Jesus cast the demons into a heard of pigs which promptly ran off of a cliff and into the lake where they drowned.

The pig herders ran into town and reported the loss of the pigs and even more amazingly, the healing of the man. The town's people came out to see for themselves. When they arrived they were startled by what they saw. There was the crazy, naked, bleeding guy but now he was clean and dressed and sitting calmly. Mark 5:15 says the people were afraid. The people began to plead with Jesus to leave their area.

There's a part of me that struggles with this passage. I want to slap the people across the face. Why would they want Jesus to leave? He had just performed an amazing miracle, demonstrated compassion, and changed this man's life forever. I can't be too hard on them. Sometimes we get scared when we see the hand of God as well. Sometimes when Jesus is moving in our lives we would just rather him stop or go somewhere else before it gets uncomfortable.

The man tried to get in the boat with Jesus but he wouldn't let him. Jesus told the man to go home, visit his family, and tell them what had happened. Imagine that homecoming. I'm pretty sure it would one-up the narrative of The Prodigal Son. Mark 5:20 says, "So the man went away and began to tell in the Decapolis how much Jesus had done for him. And all the people were amazed."

When was the last time you were so urgent about saving people's lives? Paul Rusesabagina knows what it feels like. As the Rwandan Genocide swept the African country of Rwanda in 1994, the Interahamwe militia, comprised of Hutu tribesmen, was determined to kill every member of the Tutsi tribe in the country. The distinction between the two tribes was made by the Belgians decades ago when they occupied the country. It was as simple as the tone of one's skin. Tutsis had lighter black skin than the Hutus.

The slaughter was unimaginable. Nearly 800,000 Tutsis died over the course of 10 weeks for simply having the wrong shade of skin. Any Hutu who sympathized with the Tutsis was also killed. Entire orphanages were brutally slaughtered. Women were raped and chopped in pieces by the machetes of the militia. Men were tied to trees and beaten to death. The entire genocide happened on our evening news as we sat at the dinner table wondering how something like that could happen.

Paul Rusesabagina was on the management staff of the Sebena Hotel des Mille Collines, an exclusive luxury hotel in Kigali, Rwanda. Although Rusesabagina was a Hutu he refused to take part in the massacres. His wife was a Tutsi as were many of his friends, employees, and neighbors. Rusesabagina began to bribe the militia with cash, jewelry, alcohol, and anything else he could get his hands on in order to get Tutsis and moderate Hutus into the hotel. The hotel was frequently attacked and the members of Rusesabagina's clan, including his wife and children, were brutally beaten.

Eventually, Rusesabagina managed to work a deal with the United Nations peacekeeping forces which were forbidden from intervening in the crisis to facilitate the escape of 1,268 Tutsis and moderate Hutus who sought shelter in the besieged hotel. You can watch Rusesabagina's story in the critically acclaimed film, Hotel Rwanda. Rusesabagina could have left the country several times prior to and after the violence broke out. Instead, he was determined to work to save lives in as urgent a way as possible.

When was the last time you were so passionate about the transformation in your life that you couldn't help but tell people about Jesus? I love this encounter with Jesus because of the complete transformation. One man's amazement with Jesus brings others to be awestruck as well. The people in Mark 5:20 were amazed because of the powerful testimony of the transformed life.

You see, what we do with our Jesus encounter matters. It matters to our friends. It matters to our families. It matters to those who haven't yet had their encounter.

Kenny is on fire. He joined our Launch Team for the new church about seven weeks ago. We quickly identified Kenny and his wife, Shannon, as individuals with a high quotient for leadership and influence. We had a family outreach event last weekend in which Kenny and Shannon brought nine families with them.

When was the last time you brought nine families to anything church related? My answer would be never.

Kenny and Shannon live lives that glorify God. They don't shy away from people that are different from them. They don't lecture people all day. They just love the people around them on a daily basis. And there's no doubt where that love originates. When was the last time you witnessed the sort of passion exhibited by the man in Mark 5:20?

I have to believe the disciples were amazed that day as well. It wasn't the exorcism. They had seen that before. It wasn't the amazement of the crowd. They had seen that before. It wasn't Jesus staying calm in a hair-raising situation. They had seen that before. This time, the disciples were left awestruck by the compassion of Jesus. If we look closely, we will be as well.

7

When They Thought They Had Seen It All

"Little girl, I say to you, get up!"

—Mark 5:42

"JUST WHEN you think you've seen it all." I'm from the South and that phrase carries a lot of weight and also a warning. It's at those moments of life where we think we've encountered everything that a surprise usually shatters the viewpoint into a million pieces. It can be serious. It can be comical. It's always true.

Most of these momentous occasions of life are provided by our ten year-old son, Trace. Trace has mastered the can-do American spirit at such a young age that it is literally frightening on a weekly basis to see what Trace thinks he can do. The problem for Trace is that he hasn't quite developed the counter-balance to his audacious mentality. The end result sometimes creates a great, but always amusing, chasm between good idea and bad idea. Just when I think I've seen it all, well, he gives me more material.

I'm writing looking out the window at Trace right now and I have to admit I'm halfway curious whether to let him continue one of these tasks or to stop him right now. I'm leaning towards stopping him but you have to understand the scene I'm witnessing to greatly appreciate the heights of his ingenuity that often overshadow the chasm of his fear. I think that's just a fancy way of describing ten year-old boys.

Back to the scene at hand. Trace has a basketball goal in the driveway. The backboard has worked its way loose of the frame on one side. I told Trace we would get it fixed this weekend. He's determined to take matters into his own hands.

The base of the backboard is ten feet off the ground. There's no way he can reach it. That doesn't stop Trace. He's now stacked scraps of wood into two piles. Here comes my new six-foot ladder. He's put each of the legs of the ladder on one of the wood piles. Not exactly the safest base for a ladder. Now he's headed up the ladder. Time to put an end to the ingenuity. Just when you think you've seen it all.

It wasn't a ten year-old boy that provided that sentiment for the disciples. It was a young, thirty-something itinerant preacher from the hills. The disciples loaded into the boat at the end of Mark 5 determined that they had seen it all now. After all of the healings, miraculous signs, calming of the storm, and now, the healing of the crazed, demon-possessed naked man by the tombs coupled with the sight of two thousand pigs running off the edge of a cliff into the water, the disciples firmly believed they had seen it all. The only problem was they were wrong.

Mark continues his narrative revealing that Jesus and the disciples traveled back across the lake once more. I'm sure the conversation had to be plentiful on the trip. They probably recalled the storm that nearly killed them before it was put down by the voice of Jesus. They probably wondered what could possibly greet them at the dock after their last experience with the naked demon-possessed man. Whatever lay ahead of them, it was certain they had certainly seen it all at this point. Wrong.

They could see the large crowd that was gathering around the shore as the boat began to make its approach. One man stood out. They knew Jairus as one of the leaders of the synagogue, the Jewish house of worship in the area. What happened next as Jesus departed the boat would forever serve to teach the disciples the lesson that when you walk with Jesus there's always something new and adventurous waiting around the corner.

Mark 5:22–23 says, "Seeing Jesus, he fell at his feet and pleaded earnestly with him, 'My little daughter is dying. Please come and put your hands on her so that she will be healed and live.'" In a narrative that reveals the compassionate nature of Jesus so clearly, Mark simply says in verse 24, "So Jesus went with him." Jesus responded to the man's heart-felt cry by joining him for his journey.

Meanwhile, the crowd continued to surge around Jesus as if he were a rock star fresh from the stage of a major concert venue. They pushed, shoved, and forced their way close to the newest celebrity of Galilee. The disciples became make-shift body guards in their own mind. Once during Jesus' ministry the disciples even tried to deny a group of children from approaching Jesus.

The crowd this day was simply too large to contain when it happened. Mark 5:40 says that Jesus realized that power had gone out from him. That's an amazing look into the physiological make-up of Jesus. While fully human, he was also fully God. He felt the power of his own spirit depart his body.

Mark could have said a thousand things to explain how Jesus knew something had happened. It could have been a cerebral thought process. After all, Jesus knows everything. Instead, Mark made sure to relate that Jesus felt power depart from his body.

Mark also gives us the back story on the woman to whom the power departed. She had suffered from bleeding for twelve years. Some suggest that bleeding to be a continuous menstrual cycle. Whatever it was, Mark says she had "suffered a great deal." The doctors only made things worse. She sought healing for so long. This day she knew it was coming to her once and for all.

She muscled her way through the crowd as only a determined woman could do. Have you ever seen a determined mother or grandmother on Black Friday bent on reaching the best sales in the store? Multiply that a hundred times. She knew if she could just get close enough, if she could catch his eye, if she could divert his attention, she could be his next miracle.

I wonder sometimes if we lose sight of the fact that we are God's miracles. Our lives, once tired, worn, and hopeless, are fulfilled and made complete through Jesus. Yet when the bumps of life arise, somehow we forget where to turn. Rather than finding our way to God we find our way back to whatever it was that made us tired, worn, and hopeless in the first place.

She was so sure her freedom would come from Jesus that she decided if she could just touch his cloak she would be healed. The Secret Service would have spotted her from a mile away. She reached out and touched the cloak of Jesus and instantly felt a change within her body.

Jesus searched the crowd to find the woman, as if he really need to. After all, he knew exactly who it was. Her eyes flooded with tears and her heart burst with joy as she fell at the feet of the only one in history who could set her free. She shared her story, her affliction, her pain, and the joy of her freedom. Jesus listened all the while before saying, "Daughter, your faith has healed you. Go in peace and be freed from your suffering."

A lot of us would love to be freed from our suffering. Maybe you've floated the credit cards and checking account so long that you don't know how to feed your family this month. Maybe you're in a relationship that needs to turn around in a hurry or you're not so sure it's going to last. Maybe your parent, spouse, or child received a diagnosis you never wanted to hear. As long as we live on this earth, suffering will surround us.

The problem is that so many of us reach out for dangerous coping mechanisms. You never thought you would be addicted but now your medicine cabinet looks like a pharmacy and you find yourself searching for new ways to find prescription drugs. You knew alcoholism ran in your family but you never thought it would rise up in you and now you find yourself searching the bottle for each last drop. You never thought your conversations would go anywhere. After all, you just needed someone with which to share what's going on in your marriage. Now you're starring at the alarm clock in the hotel room in the middle of the afternoon wondering how you ended up there.

We can't avoid suffering. We can avoid reaching in the wrong directions. The woman was at her last resort. She had literally tried everything. She knew there was only one last reach left within her. She reached out to Jesus. Have you?

Of course all of this was very touching for Jairus but his daughter was ill. I can imagine my thought process if I were Jairus. "Come on Jesus, this lady and her bleeding will be here tomorrow. My daughter is dying right now." "Jesus, really? She's healed already. We've got to get a move on or my daughter will die." Yet Mark never records any irritation from Jairus.

The news came suddenly. Mark 5:35 says, "While Jesus was still speaking some men came from the house of Jairus, the synagogue ruler. 'Your daughter is dead,' they said, 'Why bother the teacher any more?'" The news must have hit Jairus with a thud.

One of the greatest fears and pains to ever be experienced by any parent is the thought of losing their child. The only thing worse in this world is that actual experience coming true. This was his little girl, his princess. The pain of that thought shot through his body and must have threatened to rip his heart in two. Yet Jesus wasn't done. Jesus turned to Jairus and responded, "Don't be afraid; just believe."

Our encounters with Jesus are often found on the map at the intersection of faith and fear. Surely Jairus' friends rolled their eyes knowing there was nothing left in the scenario but fear. Yet only can we experience Jesus in the fullest way when we trade our fear for faith. Jairus was determined to be filled with faith.

They reached the house and Jesus took his trusted three inner-core disciples, Peter, James, and John, inside the home. Since Mark probably recorded Peter's eye-witness account of the event it is as accurate of a portrait as you could find as they entered the home characterized by commotion, confusion, and noise. Jesus evicted everyone but the three disciples and Jairus and his wife.

Jesus made his way to where the child was laid. He took her by the hand and said, "Little girl, I say to you, get up!" That day at the intersection of fear and faith, Jairus' daughter awoke from death. Mark 5:42 says that everyone in the room was "completely astonished."

Have you ever had one of those moments? A moment where you were completely astonished by an encounter with Jesus? A moment where you were awestruck by your experience with him? If not, you might just find it at the intersection of faith and fear.

8

More Than a Magician

"Then he climbed into the boat with them, and the wind died down. They were completely amazed, for they had not understood about the loaves; their hearts were hardened."

—Mark 6:51–52

I LOVED going to church camp as a kid. I made memories that have lasted well into my adult life. Unfortunately, most of those memories have nothing to do with lessons I heard or sermons I experienced. I can tell you who my first dorm parent was my first full week of camp. I can tell you that I won twenty-three straight carpet ball games one night before dinner.

I can tell you how I never ate fried chicken after a very bad experience one year. I recall the time I contracted pink eye and laid in bed for an entire day thinking the world was coming to a sudden and painful end. I can remember throwing things into the campfire when the counselors weren't looking. I can recall the train that used to bring out the hotdogs on the first night. I can remember the lake we used to swim in and the awful ear drops we received each day when we got out.

I could go on for pages but you really don't care. Of all the memories of camp, I can remember one lesson. That's it, just one. It happened at camp the summer before fifth grade and it shaped my imagination about Jesus forever.

We gathered on the beach by the lake. I remember being preoccupied with who I would sit by, what I would get from the canteen snack bar that evening, what would be served at dinner immediately following the lesson, and if I would get any mail that evening. I don't remember a whole lot about what the teacher said. I remember what I saw. There was a man dressed up like Jesus walking across the lake. For a minute, we were captivated with the idea of Jesus walking on water. We later found out the counselors had submerged a row of picnic tables beneath the surface at just the right height to appear as if the actor was walking on the surface of the water.

I like to imagine that when we get to Heaven there is a film room where we get to view some of the greatest moments of biblical history. I used to describe the room as being full of VHS tapes. Let's upgrade to Blue Ray discs. I want so badly to put in a disc and see the water rising around Noah's ark, the parting of the Red Sea, the collapse of Jericho's walls, David slaying Goliath, Jesus calming the storm and so many more.

One that would certainly make my short list would be the night Jesus walked on water in Mark 6:45–52. Sometimes I'm honestly not so sure what I would like to see more—Jesus walking on the surface of the water or the look on the faces of the disciples as Jesus did so. I'm sure each would be amazing.

The passage begins in such a quick way that you almost miss the nuance of the occasion which leads to the very miracle itself. Jesus had just performed one of his most memorable miracles by feeding five thousand men and their families by multiplying enough food from a simple five loaves of bread and two fish. Mark 6:45 says, "Immediately Jesus made his disciples get into the boat and go ahead of him to Bethsaida, while he dismissed the crowd." The crowd was ready to anoint Jesus as the long-awaited King following the miracle and he was determined to diffuse the situation by sending his disciples in one direction and the crowd in another.

Mark then records that Jesus went up on a mountainside to pray. Mark 6:47 says, "When evening came, the boat was in the middle of the lake, and he was alone on the land. He saw the disciples straining at the oars, because the wind was against them." The disciples were surely frightened as they fought the storm. The last time they faced such a fury, Jesus calmed the storm with nothing but the sound of his voice. Now, he wasn't with them.

After watching for a while, Jesus decided to walk out to the boat. Mark says that as Jesus was about to pass by the boat they saw him for the first time and thought he was a ghost. The disciples were terrified. Jesus called out to the boat in Mark 6:50, "Take courage! It is I. Don't be afraid." My paraphrase would read something like this: "What's the big deal? Haven't you ever seen the creator of the universe walk on water before?"

I'm convinced that Jesus had a sense of humor. I'd love to know what the campfire conversations were like at the end of each day during his ministry journeys. I wish we had a little more insight into the practical jokes of thirteen men traveling the wilderness from stressful location to location over a three year period. Despite lacking that information, Mark does provide us with this situation where Jesus' humor shines through.

He climbed in to the boat and the wind died down. Mark then provides a haunting statement in Mark 6:52, "[The disciples] were completely amazed, for they had not understood about the loaves; their hearts were hardened." Is it possible to witness the miraculous and not be moved? It is possible to encounter greatness and come away without being awestruck? According to Mark it was then and it is now.

The disciples had just witnessed one of the most amazing and signature miracles of Jesus' ministry on earth. Yet the multiplication of the loaves stood just as a simple magic trick instead of the actual revelation of the identity of the King of Kings. They missed the identity of Jesus.

We do the same thing. We all hold different viewpoints of Jesus for different times in our life. We have the get-out-of-jail-free Jesus for when things look the bleakest. We have the give-me-a-miracle-now-because-I-really-need-it Jesus for when we don't know where to turn. Our kids have the I-really-didn't-study-but-bless-me-with-amazing-knowledge Jesus on test day. The end result is that we cheapen the actual identity of Jesus.

Jesus didn't come to us as a magic rabbit's foot to be kept in our pocket for good luck. Jesus didn't come to us as a magic eight ball to give us a "yes, no, or maybe." Jesus didn't come to us as some sort of cosmic insurance. Jesus came to us as the God of the universe. Paul says in Colossians 1:17, "He is before all things, and in him all things hold together."

Instead of appreciating the fullness and indescribable greatness of the identity of Jesus we've managed to turn him into some sort of Santa Clause. We turn to him once or twice a year when we know what we really want him to produce for our pleasure. The end result is we fail to notice him when the waves rise and winds crash. We wonder what we could possibly be mistaking for an individual at work in our lives. After all, it must simply be a ghost of our imagination.

On the other hand, when Jesus becomes so real that he walks across the waves of our life amidst the blowing winds and we recognize him for who he is, we encounter him in the way that he meant for us to meet him in the first place. Jesus never intended for us to compartmentalize him or place him in any of the boxes that we do as humans. He knew we would from time to time. He also knew we could rise above that minimization.

The thing that scares me the most about the passage is that Mark says the disciples "hearts were hardened." These were the same disciples that witnessed the feeding of the five thousand, the resurrection of the dead girl, and not to mention, Jesus showing his power in calming another storm on the sea. These were the same disciples who woke up each day next to him around the fire.

These were the same disciples who listened to his teaching and followed his path each day.

The disciples were surrounded by those approaching Jesus with a consumer mentality. They came to Jesus because of what he could give them. Sometimes it was sight, hearing, clean skin, freedom from illness, even life itself. Very seldom did the disciples witness anyone come to Jesus because of who he was, rather they came for what he could give.

If you lean in closely to that line of thought it can start to sound a lot like the American church. While Christians around the world in places like China, Sudan, Iran, and Iraq, face death each week for their allegiance to Jesus, we simply face inconveniences like missing soccer games and giving up an hour of sleep. I wonder how many of us each week approach our relationship with what Jesus can do for us without ever considering what it is that we can and should offer to him.

You should know who Shaun King is if you don't already. While I don't know Shaun personally, I've followed his blog and church plant, The Courageous Church, in urban Atlanta for quite some time. Courageous is a church determined to recognize and reflect the identity of Jesus rather than presenting simply another consumer-driven community.

Shaun was in the news most recently for his project that garnered the support of more than 100 celebrities, from Eva Longoria to Ryan Seacrest to Emmitt Smith, called aHomeInHaiti .org. Remember the devastation in Haiti? We cared about that a year ago. Courageous Church still cares. In fact, they care so much that even CNN took note of their caring a few months ago featuring them on their broadcast and nominating Shaun as a person of the year.

The earthquake that rattled Haiti left it with little to no infrastructure whatsoever as the people prepared to face the devastating Hurricane season. aHomeInHaiti.org is an initiative started by King to raise money to supply simple tents to provide shelter from the pelting of the rainy season in Haiti. The effort has been featured on FOX News, CNN, NBC, and more media outlets who marvel at a church truly caring for hurting people.

While I'm so encouraged for what has been and will continue to be accomplished through Courageous Church and aHomeIn-Haiti.org, it breaks my heart that such an initiative by a church is ground-breaking to national news outlets. Have we become so inward, consumer focused that we no longer recognize our true identity as the light of the world because we've somehow lost focus of the true identity of the one whom we gather to celebrate?

We should expect the amazing from Jesus. We should expect him to meet us where we are. We should expect him to show up in our lives on a daily basis. When we reach that point, we'll stop seeing crazy coincidences and be left awestruck by the creator of the universe who cares enough to show up in our lives down here.

9

On the Mountain

"There he was transfigured before them. His clothes became
dazzling white, whiter than anyone in the world could bleach
them. And there appeared before them Elijah and Moses, who
were talking with Jesus."

—Mark 9:2

W E HEADED up the mountain full of excitement. I was a
young student pastor with absolutely zero experience. In
fact, if I had the opportunity to interview myself at that age and
experience now there's no way I would hire me. Nevertheless, we
were armed with enthusiasm and vague directions as we headed up
the mountain. Our school bus converted to a church bus chugged
along nicely as we drove. We sold the fifteen passenger church van
in order to find a vehicle which was both safer and able to haul our
entire group on trips.

A friend of mine from the Tri-County Tennessee area recom-
mended we explore a waterfall hidden deep in the woods at the top
of the mountain. I wasn't quite so sure we would ever see the waterfall but it seemed like a worthy cause. And so, we marched. We
marched across the field. We marched into the woods. We marched
deeper into the woods where the path stopped and became a trail.
We marched to the end of the trail where we were faced with the
option of continuing with no trail or turning back.

We stopped at the last scenic overlook marked on the path to discuss our options and see if we could see, hear, or otherwise sense the approaching waterfall of the promise. Although I was young and ignorant, I recognized the inherent risks represented in the side of a mountain. I encouraged our students to move back from the rails, stay away from the edges, and generally not too breathe. That's when it happened.

I heard the scream followed by the sound of broken branches followed by the sound of more broken branches. I instantly imagined the phone call to a parent informing them the worst had happened to their child under my care on the side of a mountain on a remote trail in east Tennessee. I rushed to the broken rail and looked down to see her lying on her back on a rock some 25 feet beneath the observation deck. To my surprise, it wasn't one of the students from our group, it was one of our adult sponsors. To make things even worse, she was the mother of two of our students who were now hysterically screaming at the thought and image of their mother following the fall.

I made my way down the slope with one of our other adult sponsors while adults tried to move students away from the ledge. We started slowly examining pain and movement but found out very quickly that our friend was going to be fine and had suffered only minor scrapes from the branches on the way down. We let out a sigh of relief, shared a laugh, and began to climb back up to the rest of the group. Our group spent time hugging and praising God. We went down the mountain a different group than we when ascended.

Peter, James, and John understood what it was like to have a life-altering encounter on the mountain top. They went up a mountain one day with Jesus only to see him in an entirely new light that they could have ever imagined. This trip up the mountain left everyone involved changed.

Mark's narrative reveals that Jesus' ministry was at the height of success. Thousands were gathering to hear him, even following him from point to point and swarming the hillside to hear his next teaching or see his next miracle. Despite the fact that Jesus had become somewhat of a traveling celebrity, he pulled the disciples aside in Mark 8 to have an uncomfortable conversation in predicting his death.

A week after dropping that bombshell on his closest of friends and followers he took Peter, James, and John with him and led them up a high mountain in Mark 9:2. Mark then levels one of the most understated verses in all of Scripture that you all most miss if you blink or get tempted to scan through the passage, "There [Jesus] was transfigured before them." Maybe we miss it because *transfigure* isn't a word we use on a regular basis.

Transfigure—v. to change in outward appearance, to transform

Jesus was physically transformed before their very eyes. His wardrobe was even affected. Mark says, "His clothes became dazzling white, whiter than anyone in the world could bleach them." Peter, James, and John had witnessed so many amazing moments with Jesus. They had front row seats to his greatest teachings, healings, and miracles. This, however, was unlike anything they had seen to this point.

Mark then slips another verse in that is easy to gloss over, "And there appeared before them Elijah and Moses, who were talking with Jesus." Two of the greatest, best-known Jewish celebrities of the faith, dead for hundreds of years, emerged on top of the mountain to chit-chat with Jesus. Peter was in awe:

[Peter] said to Jesus, "Rabbi it is good for us to be here. Let us put up three shelters—one for you, one for Moses, and one for Elijah."

Mark almost feels sorry for Peter as he records Peter's memories of the day under the inspiration of the Holy Spirit and adds that Peter had no earthly idea what to say because he was so frightened. After all, Peter had the gift of filling an awkward or uncomfortable moment with his gift of gab. If ever there was one individual in Scripture who held the record for inserting their foot in their mouth the most frequently, Peter would be nominated for first, second, and third place.

Peter couldn't help but attempt to spiritualize his own presence in the group. He wanted to make clear a distinction was made. "It is good for *us* to be here." Notice he didn't say, "I wish everybody else was here for this." "I wish Andrew could see this now." Instead, Peter wanted to make it clear he approved of his presence.

Peter also had the gift for missing the point at inopportune times. He desired to construct three tents—one for Moses, one for Elijah, and one for Jesus. I know the text order is different but I'm pretty convinced this was how Peter approached his thought process. After all, Moses and Elijah were royalties of the faith. Jesus was an upstart with a good couple of years under his belt.

God took the opportunity to clear up any confusion of roles and importance. "This is my Son, whom I love. Listen to him!" In translation for Peter, Jesus matters more and outranks Moses and Elijah. We don't get the full effect of that sentiment but Peter, James, and John would have been rocked to their core. They studied Moses and Elijah from an early age and now they had met them personally only to find out that their childhood heroes of the faith ranked far less superior than the man they followed on a daily basis. Their viewpoint of Jesus' physical appearance wasn't the only thing transformed on the mountain that day. Then, as quickly as they arrived, Moses and Elijah were gone and all was back to normal.

As they walked down the mountain, Jesus gave distinct instructions. Mark 9:9–10 says, "As they were coming down the mountain, Jesus gave them orders not to tell anyone what they had seen until the Son of Man had risen from the dead. They kept the matter to themselves, discussing what "rising from the dead" meant."

How could someone rise from the dead? Who is this man that we are traveling the countryside with? Is he more than just a good teacher and worker of wonders? They knew one thing for sure, he was greater than both Moses and Elijah.

It's easy sometimes to blast the questions of the disciples, especially the inner-core of Peter, James, and John. But if we're being honest, don't we struggle with the same questions? What do we do with Jesus? Who is this man? Is he a man? Can someone really rise form the dead? Was he more than just a good teacher or magician?

As we descend down the mountain with Peter, James, and John in Mark 9, we're left awestruck at the identity and wonder of the identity of Jesus. Mark gives us a moment to catch our breath and realize that our amazement is not always found in what Jesus does, but rather in who Jesus is. The very root of his greatness revolves around his identity. For a brief moment on the mountain that day, Peter, James, and John were able to marvel at both the identity and ability of Jesus.

Sometimes we struggle to truly understand Jesus. It's nothing new. The early First and Second Century Church leaders had to fight a false doctrine called Gnosticism which was rooted in a misunderstanding of Jesus that was nearly as dangerous to the longevity of Jesus' movement as was the thought of persecution. The Gnostics argued that God was divine, perfect, and pure and that the human body was carnal, ravaged, depraved, and torn. The Gnostics argued that Jesus couldn't possibly have been both God and man as the two elements could not exist together. The argument threatened to tear the church at its seams.

We struggle with the identity of Jesus in much the same way today in our society. Maybe he was just a good teacher. Maybe he was a gifted illusionist. Maybe he was crazy. But then again, maybe he was who he said he was. C. S. Lewis, one of the greatest philosophers and defenders of Christianity in modern times, argued that when faced with the questions of Jesus we are left with only three options. Jesus was either crazy, a liar, or he really was God.

Peter, James, and John had no doubt that day as they descended the mountain together. It was a crucial moment for Peter as he retold the story to Mark. It was a moment that shaped the rest of their lives; lives that would lead to death for Peter and James and exile for John. Sometimes I wonder how the disciples could have been filled with so much faith to face the hardships they endured due to their faith in Jesus. I think it's because they saw Jesus on the mountaintop for who he really was and is still today. Will you?

10

The Choice

"At this the man's face fell. He went away sad, because he had
great wealth."

—Mark 10:22

I was never cut out for Children's Ministry. I don't communicate
well on their level and would never remember the myriad of
rules that have to be established and maintained in order to have
a successful ministry to children. My wife, on the other hand,
spent a very successful decade serving vocationally in Children's
Ministry and still volunteers in the ministry at our church. One of
the beauties of having a wife in Children's Ministry is that you have
the *blessing* of volunteering in the pint-sized world.

Before we go any further, I have nothing against kids. I love
my three. I would probably think highly of yours as well and I happen to believe that ministering to our children is one of the most
important tasks in which parents and churches can ever partner.
It's just not my calling in ministry. Nevertheless, I served when my
wife was working and received more out of the equation than I ever
put in. I'm a firm believer of volunteering in Children's Ministry.

With the disclaimer out the way, I must admit I'm a hor-
rible classroom leader for pre-school children. That's not a secret.
Everyone knows it. I'm a good assistant, just not cut out for the
head honcho role in the classroom.

It was Summer Vacation Bible School and our building was full of wide-eyed children soaking up God's love as if they were sponges. My job usually consisted of placing my un-incredible thespian skills on display during the opening skits in order to drive home the main point of the evening. After that, my job title was officially, "Floater." I think that meant snack taster.

One particular evening I was helping a pre-school class in which the assistant was ill and failed to show up. Things were going well and it was time to leave the movie room to return to our class-room for snack. In order to keep the pre-school children moving in the right direction the teacher extended a rope and had everyone grab a spot. We walked down the hallway without incident with the rope serving as our guide to keep us together and in line.

We reached the classroom and instructed the children to sit around the tables for their snacks. I heard the commotion behind me and turned to realize that one of the children was refusing to let go of the rope. As a matter of fact, he had wadded the entire rope up into a ball and was standing in the corner with the rope. This must have been of deep concern to the other children because they were screaming that the child was stilling holding the rope.

I approached the young boy with his snack bowl in my hand and asked for the rope. I figured we could make a deal. After all, who wouldn't want to trade a dirty, frayed rope for a bowl full of goldfish crackers. This boy, that's who. I continued to reason with the child. I offered my best logic as to why it was in his best interest to accept my goldfish, let go of the rope, and sit in his chair. No matter what I said, he refused to let go of the rope.

I think we're determined to hang on to a lot of things in life. God tries to remind us of his blessings if we would just let go of the rope. No matter how rational the thought process, we refuse to let go. We keep hanging on.

Maybe that's why I find one of Jesus' encounters in Mark to be one of the most disturbing interactions of his ministry personally. It's because I can see myself refusing to let go of the rope. I see myself gripping with white knuckles to hold on to all that is dear to me and refusing all that is dear to him.

In Mark 10 a man approaches and throws himself at the feet of Jesus. "Good teacher," he asked, "what must I do to inherit eternal life?" We know a couple of facts about the man. First, Matthew, Mark, and Luke record that the man was rich. Second, Matthew records that the man was young (Matthew 19:20).

Jesus decided to use the moment for a teaching opportunity. "Why do you call me good?" Jesus answered. It was extremely uncommon in Jewish culture to call someone good. The expression was reserved only for God. It was highly irregular for someone to use the expression towards another individual and certainly would have made even the disciples uncomfortable.

Jesus turned the discussion towards the commandments received by Moses and instilled on the hearts of every Jewish boy. Interestingly, Jesus doesn't start with the first grouping of commandments which dwell on man's relationship with God. Instead, he dwells on the commandments focusing on the relationships between humans.

The young man is quick to point out that he has observed and kept every letter of the law since he was a boy. At the age of thirteen the young man would have become a bar mitzvah (son of the commandment). It was at that occasion of life that the young man would have taken upon himself to keep the commandments and obey the law.

Despite the overall sadness of the passage, I love Mark 10:21. "Jesus looked at him and loved him." Did you catch that? When Jesus looks at us he loves us! You are loved by the creator of the universe. You are loved by the one who spoke light into existence. You are loved by the one who designed the sun, moon, and stars. You are loved by the God of the universe!

"One thing you lack," Jesus said. "Go, sell everything you have and give to the poor, and you will have treasure in heaven. Then come, follow me." Jesus never meant for following him to be a simple proposition. It was never supposed to be a simple choice. It was never supposed to be the easy path.

Maybe it was even more of a difficult proposition for this young man because he was wealthy with a vast estate. Mark 10:22 says, "At this the man's face fell. He went away sad, because he had great wealth." Jesus turned to his disciples and said, "How hard is it for the rich to enter the kingdom of God!"

The honest truth is that the man simply didn't expect that response from Jesus. Jewish culture valued wealth. Wealth was viewed upon as a sign of God's divine appointment or an indication of piety. Poverty was viewed as the same divine symbol in the opposite direction.

Jesus' teaching was revolutionary and challenged every fiber of the young man's spiritual being. He couldn't imagine doing away with his wealth. What would people think about him? Who would provide for him? He couldn't let go of his rope no matter what Jesus was offering. He was determined to hold on and so he turned and walked away sad.

Sometimes it's not so much what we are holding on to as much as it is what is holding on to us. As I'm finishing the final rewrites of this book it's impossible to ignore the story of Ted Williams. Perhaps you've noticed. If not, well, come out from under your rock to experience the feel good story of the year (and it's only January).

Ted Williams is the homeless man with the golden voice for radio. A reporter for a local Columbus, Ohio, newspaper saw Williams panhandling near an intersection and asked him to speak to the camera in his radio voice for a dollar. The rest, as they say, is history. The video found its way onto YouTube and received more than four million views in less than three days.

Job offers for voiceover work began to flood for Williams to provide a way off of the streets. How could such a natural talent end up working street corners for quarters with disheveled hair, patched clothing, and starving? The story began to emerge.

Williams once held a job as a radio personality and voiceover artist. He introduced illegal drugs into his life and soon found himself battling a serious addiction. He lost his job. He lost his next job and the next. More importantly, he lost his relationship with his aging mother, wife, and three children. He's never met his grandchildren. He lost all of it because of what had a hold on him.

I say all of that because it's really easy to make this passage some sort of pronouncement against wealthy people. That really wasn't Jesus' intent. Money just happened to be what Jesus was calling this man to forfeit in return for becoming one of his followers. It could be a number of things to us. Maybe it's athletics for you. Maybe it's an inappropriate relationship. Maybe it's food. Maybe it's alcohol. Maybe it's your career. Whatever it is within us, we can never truly follow Jesus until we give up everything else and place him on the top shelf.

I wonder what would have happened if the young man would have simply written a check, liquidated the account, given it to the poor, and reported back to Jesus. I wonder what would have happened if the man would have become a follower of Jesus. Would we know his name? Would we know his story? Would God have used him to do something great for his Kingdom? I think the answer to all of those questions is a resounding yes. Yet none of that matters since the man was unable to reshuffle his priorities of life.

Are you in that conversation right now? What is God calling you to give up? Is he waiting for you to make the decision so that you can make him famous by serving his Kingdom? One thing we know for sure, if you choose to walk away, you'll never know.

11

When It Gets Hard

"'Am I leading a rebellion,' said Jesus, 'that you have come out with swords and clubs to capture me? Every day I was with you, teaching in the temple courts, and you did not arrest me. But the Scriptures must be fulfilled.' Then everyone deserted him and fled."

—Mark 14:48–50

WE WERE on the interstate and there weren't a whole lot of options for a birthday meal as we traveled back to Kentucky from a week of magic at Walt Disney World in Orlando, Florida. Our youngest daughter, Lilly Grace, was turning three that day as we drove and we were determined she have a birthday meal. The best thing we could find was a Pizza Hut in a small southern Tennessee town. We set the GPS and headed to the birthday dinner.

Once we had ordered I decided to check out the juke box in the corner. You don't see too many of those anymore. As a matter of fact, our ten year-old, Trace, had no clue what it was. We searched through the song list and I knew I had the perfect selection. Our oldest child, Makayla, was a huge fan of a certain teenage heartthrob which seemed to be wooing the hearts of young girls across the nation. Being the cool dad I am, I quickly selected three straight songs from the artist and returned to the table.

I was so excited about the surprise that I was determined not to tell Makayla what I had done until she got excited when the first song of her favorite artist began to play. Two *Freebirds* and a *Back In Black* later and it was time for what was sure to be her favorite set-list to begin. I was so excited I could hardly stand it. Then, it began.

"Can you believe someone would pick this song?" Makayla sighed as the speakers began to croon the hit of the teen heartthrob. Then it hit her, I spent a long time at the juke box. "Did you pick this song?" I prepared for my defense and cross-examination.

"This is your favorite artist! You love this song!" I blurted.

What came next was her response that I promise I couldn't make up if I tried. "He was my favorite artist last month. I hate that song now." Lesson learned. Don't select him on the juke box again.

We've all seen it happen. Each generation has pop-stars rise to such popularity that it almost seems like they're afforded different standards for life than anyone else. Eventually the fans grow less fanatical and the crowds thin. Alas, fame is fleeting and most of these one-hit wonders end up on a VH1 Where Are They Now special five years later begging for another fifteen minutes of fame.

While Jesus didn't spend much time in the recording studio, he did experience a meteoric rise to stardom. Crowds gathered to follow his appearances and journeys in such great mass that it was nearly impossible to even get near the carpenter's son from Nazareth. Yet, the crowds couldn't last forever.

Jesus had a difficult message. Deny yourself and follow him.

Jesus had a bold statement. He was the Son of God.

Jesus had a disappointed fan base. It grew increasingly apparent that Jesus would never lead a military revolt against the Roman occupation of Palestine.

Jesus had impatient followers. If only they could force his hand to reveal his true power in a desperate time.

Jesus had powerful enemies. He had to be stopped. His teaching was dangerous to the religious status quo. If people followed him, their religion would be different.

All of these added up to take a toll on the followers of Jesus especially during the last week of his life. Mark devotes a great percentage of his work to that final week of Jesus' life. I think that's because Peter remembered that week vividly. It was etched on his soul. At times it haunted him. At times it gave him hope.

The final week of Jesus' life was filled with ups and downs. It began as he entered the city of Jerusalem as a pop star with crowds lining the streets to celebrate his arrival. It ended as he was led through the very same streets as a convicted criminal being marched to the place of his death. It included a deeply intimate meal with his closest friends. It also included betrayal by one of his closest. For all of the ups and downs that Jesus experienced that week, Peter experienced them at ground zero.

Peter watched at eye-level as the God of the Universe experienced pain, betrayal, torture, and death for us. The final week in the life of Jesus presented an emotional rollercoaster for Peter beginning in his final meal with Jesus as he pledged his undying allegiance. Jesus predicted his betrayal to the disciples as they gathered for their last meal together. Jesus predicted that not only would he be betrayed, all of the disciples would fall away as well. Mark records Peter's dramatic oath of allegiance in verse 29, "Even if all fall away, I will not."

Jesus knew better. In Mark 14:30, Jesus replied to Peter, "I tell you the truth, today—yes, tonight—before the rooster crows twice you yourself will disown me three times." Peter couldn't believe it. He responded back in his typical macho-egotistical voice, "Even if I have to die with you, I will never disown you." Never is a long time.

The night progressed and Peter found himself as one of the inner circle of Jesus' followers praying in the garden. Jesus instructed Peter, James, and John to keep watch as they prayed. He returned twice to find them sleeping. Peter must have felt so inferior but he never could have anticipated where his night would lead.

Judas arrived with the Temple guard to arrest Jesus. Mark 14:44 says, "Now the betrayer had arranged a signal with [the guard]: 'The one I kiss is the man; arrest him and lead him away under guard.'" Mark doesn't even give Judas the dignity of his name. He calls him "the betrayer."

It all seemed to happen so fast. Mark records in verse 47 that "one of those standing near drew his sword and struck the servant of the high priest, cutting off his ear." As much as Mark wished to denigrate Judas by not using his name, he offered a chance of anonymity for Peter in not identifying him as the swordsman. John 18:10 provides Peter as the sword-wielding disciple and Malchus as the afflicted servant. Jesus immediately reached down and restored the ear as commotion appeared to be ready to envelope the scene.

Jesus asked the guards, "Am I leading a rebellion that you have come out with swords and clubs to capture me?" Everyone knew the answer to the question. Everyone also knew the direction the evening was headed. Panic filled the disciples and Mark 14:50 says, "Then everyone deserted him and fled."

That's a grave thought if you pause to consider it. I'll be honest and say that I've missed that verse for years as I look at this passage. It's not so much that I've missed the fact that the disciples scattered and ran into the darkness. I missed the fact that in an instance there we are in Scripture.

How often do we choose to desert Jesus and flee from him? Unfortunately, the answer is probably far too often. I used to have this magical view of life as a follower of Jesus. I hoped that somehow since I made the decision to follow Jesus that he would give me some sort of super-human strength to resist temptation, some sort of super-sonic speed to flee my evil thoughts. I'm still looking for it. The fact of the matter is that the temptation to walk away from Jesus is there more often than we want to admit.

It's not always so easy to recognize.

It's the moment where you realize a stroke of the key or a push of the eraser could make a big difference in your income tax return. Besides, what are the chances they could actually catch you?

It's the moment when you realize that you're all alone and your mind begins to race to thoughts that you know don't honor God. But seriously, you're not hurting anyone.

It's the moment when the harsh response is so much easier and definitely more gratifying than the calm reply. Don't you deserve it? You worked hard all day.

It's the moment when it would be so much easier to just pack up and walk away. No one told you that it would be this hard. Isn't it time to finally do something for you?

Instead of those moments being non-existent for followers of Jesus, I'm convinced they come more often. When Peter was struggling to stay awake in the Garden, Jesus awoke him in Mark 14:37 saying, "Simon, are you asleep? Could you not keep watch for one hour? Watch and pray so that you will not fall into temptation. The spirit is willing, but the body is weak." Boy, is the body weak sometimes. Yet, there is hope for each of those moments.

Peter surely remembered the prediction of Jesus that he would deny him that evening. Was this what Jesus was talking about? Surely he could do better than this. He wouldn't let this happen again. This time he was serious. Ever been there? There is hope for those moments.

Peter found himself in the Temple courts as Jesus' trial began when one of the servant girls recognized him as he was warming by the fire. She had probably seen Jesus teach. Maybe she even witnessed a miracle. For whatever reason, she recognized Peter as one of Jesus' followers, "You also were with that Nazarene, Jesus." Peter mumbled a denial and walked outside.

The servant girl was not to be denied. She pursued Peter outside and gathered a crowd as she continued to lay claim that Peter was one of Jesus' followers. A crowd which just a week earlier celebrated Jesus' arrival in town was now ready to dismiss anyone associated with him. Peter denied his relationship with Jesus twice more as he was surely fearful for his personal safety.

Peter denied Jesus so strongly that Mark 14:71 says, "He began to call down curses on himself, and he swore to them, 'I don't know this man you're talking about.'" At that very moment the rooster crowed and Peter fulfilled Jesus' prophecy from the night before.

He was crushed. Mark 14:72 ends the passage saying that Peter "broke down and wept." Have you been there? Have you felt the disappointment in knowing you disappointed Jesus? Have you felt that moment knowing that you let him down?

Just as I didn't understand for a long time that we're not immune to sin just because we follow Jesus, I also didn't fully understand his response to our sin. Once I realized that sin was very much still in the mix and that Satan even pursues us harder when we follow Jesus it began to warp my view of God. Was God some sort of cosmic traffic cop sitting in the bushes waiting for us to do forty-two in a thirty-five with pre-filled traffic tickets ready to distribute? Was God some sort of executioner waiting for the first slip-up to lead us to the gallows?

The beauty of Peter's experience in the final week of Jesus' life is that God still used him.

Despite deserting him and fleeing into the darkness.

Despite denying him three times.

Despite cursing to prove his separation from Jesus.

God still used Peter.

The real beauty—God still wants to use us as well. God wants to use us despite the moments we flee his presence. It wasn't until I came to that realization that I began to find a true beauty in my relationship with God.

God isn't a cosmic traffic cop or a sadistic executioner. No, I began to realize that God is like my parents. My parents loved me unconditionally. I can remember times when I disappointed them. I can feel the pain now. The look on their face was never one of anger. The look on their faces was a look of sadness for me. They loved me through my mistakes. They loved me despite my mistakes. The bottom line is that my parents loved me. My God does too.

12

Faith of Our Fathers

"A certain man from Cyrene, Simon, the father of Alexander and Rufus . . ."

—Mark 15:21

IT WAS the first time I can remember ever seeing my dad cry. It's not that he doesn't cry, it's just that it was the first time I saw him overcome with grief. He didn't know the man. He had never met him.

My dad was driving to church one night when a pick-up truck in front of him began driving erratically. It was clear something was wrong. The truck was full of college-aged men, with several riding in the bed of the truck. As the truck began to skid, dad realized the situation would become grave in a hurry.

As the truck flipped twice into the ditch dad did what any of us would have done. He pulled over and rushed to the scene. Two things filled the scene—the smell of alcohol and absolute carnage. Crowds of onlookers began to arrive to attempt to rescue and assist those involved in the accident.

One of the young men was unconscious and wasn't breathing. My dad was certified in CPR and began to work on the young man immediately along with a couple of others who happened to arrive around the same time. They worked until the paramedics arrived. They never succeeded in resuscitating the young man as he died there on the side of the road in their arms.

That was the first time I remember seeing my dad cry. He cried over the loss of a life in a senseless way. He cried because of his feeling of helplessness at the scene. I remember the deep emotion of the night.

Kids tend to pick-up on the emotions of their parents. Stressed? Your kids know it. Depressed? Your kids know it. Ecstatic? Your kids know it. Heartbroken? Your kids know it.

Maybe for that reason, I'm drawn to Alexander and Rufus. If you blink while scanning Mark's narrative of the life of Jesus you'll miss them. We don't preach sermons about them. They don't show up on the topics of the newest Fall book release schedule. We don't spend a lot of time with Alexander and Rufus yet they had such an amazing and life-altering encounter with Jesus.

Their encounter was lived through their father, Simon from Cyrene. Mark's only mention of the two comes in Mark 15:21, "A certain man from Cyrene, Simon, the father of Alexander and Rufus, was passing by on his way in from the country, and they forced him to carry the cross." That's it. Nothing more.

Jesus' disciples had long deserted him after his arrest and during his multiple trials. Upon his conviction, Jesus was led through the streets, carrying his own cross, towards the place of his execution. Jesus was weak. He endured the maximum lashing with a whip which contained shards of glass and bone, designed to latch onto the skin of his back and remove the flesh and portions of muscle.

The Romans were masters of torture and execution and knew this would make the cross extremely painful. The torture also ensured that the march to the cross would be as excruciating as possible as the splintered wood of the cross rubbed the bare muscle and tissue of the back and shoulders. Throw in the fact that Jesus' beating was probably even more heinous due to the controversy surrounding him and you can understand how painful his march to the cross must have been. On top of the physical pain, there was no one to assist him. His friends had fled. His supporters had dwindled. Jesus was literally on his own as he marched towards what Mark calls Golgotha, the Place of the Skull, where the crucifixion would take place.

It was at that painful moment along the road that the Roman guards reached for someone in the crowd to help carry the load of the cross. They found Simon from Cyrene. Simon had traveled from his home of Cyrene to Jerusalem for the Passover Feast. At first glance it doesn't seem like such an important reference. Anybody could have carried the cross. Yet, Matthew, Mark, and Luke, each mention Simon of Cyrene by name.

It's safe to assume that Simon was deeply moved by the experience. What he saw, heard, and felt that day must have had an immense impact on the rest of his life. It's also safe to assume that Simon became a follower of Jesus. Why else would the gospel writers know and include his name in the narrative?

As much as the incident moved Simon, it must have impacted his children, Alexander and Rufus. Mark is the only writer to mention Simon's children. The children were undoubtedly moved by their father's portrayal of the event. I have to believe Simon choked up around the dinner table as he told the story of his weekend in Jerusalem which included the march to the cross, the crucifixion of Jesus, and the news around town just three days later that Jesus was alive again. His emotions ranged from sadness to confusion to joy. Alexander and Rufus hung on every word.

The instance not only changed Simon of Cyrene but it likely changed his entire family. There's a reason that Mark included the names of Alexander and Rufus while no one else did. Mark's work was especially geared towards connecting with the Roman reader. It was likely used by the Roman church which was led by none other than the eyewitness who supplied Mark's narrative, Peter.

The Apostle Paul wrote a letter to the church in Rome. At the end of the letter, in Romans 16:13, we find this greeting, "Greet

Rufus, chosen in the Lord, and his mother, who has been a mother to me, too." Early church fathers and leaders believed that Rufus to be the same Rufus who learned of Jesus from the experience of his father, Simon of Cyrene. Rufus was apparently not the only family member moved by the testimony as Paul mentions his mother as well.

All of that makes me a bit uncomfortable. You see, the role of a parent is incredibly important in the spiritual formation of the child. Ricky Gervais made himself a household name when he hosted the Golden Globe Awards for those not already familiar with the long-time stand-up comedian. While angering several celebrities with personal jokes during his stint as the host of the awards show he also closed the evening with his declaration of atheism.

It was nothing new for those familiar with Gervais. His atheism tends to rise to the top of his conversations frequently. In fact, he wrote an article in The Wall Street Journal, entitled "A Holiday Message From Ricky Gervais", chronicling his path to atheism as a child, which was published on December 19, 2010. Gervais describes his childhood as one deeply rooted in Christian faith. He says he adored Jesus. He even considered Jesus to be his superhero.

One day as he was drawing pictures of Jesus in his family's kitchen, his older brother approached and asked why he would spend so much time believing in Jesus. Gervais asked his mother why he should believe in Jesus. Her stammering, mumbling, moment of awkwardness supplied all the information that Gervais needed. He determined if there was no reason to believe, he wouldn't believe. It was that simple. At the age of eight years-old he became an atheist.

What happens when we as parents have the opportunity to engage important questions and dialogue with our children about their faith and we have nothing to work with? A life of disbelief if we're not careful. Our church, Momentum Christian Church, wants to strengthen parents and children to engage the faith journey together. We'll provide the elements to do just that on a weekly basis in an easy to understand way. I feel blessed to have had that experience with my parents growing up.

When we're growing up we see our dad as superman. He can leap tall buildings, run faster than a speeding bullet, and in general, hurdle the obstacles of life. As we get older we find out that no one is exempt from the pains of life, not even our dad. It's the faith I see in my dad at times like that which make him more like superman than any superhuman strength ever could.

For the last decade of my life I've been blessed to share the ups and downs of ministry with my dad. My prayer is that we will continue to share the journey for years to come. With my 11 years of ministry experience and his 40 years of ministry experience, I have drawn on his wisdom many times.

I've witnessed dad bring healing and vision in times of extreme pain in the lives of more than one church. I've witnessed dad bring the healing power of Jesus to many a fragmented life. I've also witnessed my dad go through some tough times. He's handled each with grace and faithful perseverance. I've been blessed to have a father who has modeled integrity, honor, purity, and possessed a God-honoring spirit. While the lessons I've learned from ministry have meant so much, it's the lessons of the rest of life which will resonate for years to come.

Maybe my dad can't leap tall buildings. Maybe my dad can't stop speeding trains. Maybe my dad can't run faster than a speeding bullet. None of that matters as much as I get older. What matters is not that he's superman, but that he's a super man of God.

What will your children get from you about Jesus? What will you tell them around the dinner table? Will your life match what you say? I think Mark mentions Alexander and Rufus for a very distinct reason. Not only do children matter, but parents matter as well. It's my prayer that I'll have an impact like Simon of Cyrene. Will you?

13

What Do You Do with Him?

"Surely this man was the Son of God!"

—Mark 15:39

You're not supposed to know the umpire's name. I don't know Jim Joyce. I know his name is synonymous with one of the most controversial calls in all of baseball during the 2010 season as a call at first base cost a young pitcher a chance at a perfect game on the last out of the game.

It's not like Joyce is an inexperienced umpire. Jim Joyce has two decades of experience as a Major League Baseball Umpire. He has umpired two All-Star Games, six Divisional Playoff Series, three League Championship Series, and two World Series. He was voted by Major League Baseball players as the second highest ranked umpire in the Major League last year in a poll conducted by Sports Illustrated.

None of that seems to have meant much that evening as Joyce now stood convicted of one of the most heinous mistaken calls in Major League Baseball history. Armando Galarraga stood just one out away from completing an elusive perfect game for the Detroit Tigers. A perfect game is when a pitcher keeps the other team from reaching the base in any way for the entire nine inning duration of the game. It's an extremely rare accomplishment.

Just one out separated Galarraga and his perfect game. He began the wind-up, delivered the pitch, and watched as a routine ground ball was hit into the infield. It was a close play at first base but it appeared to both the naked eye and the camera to be an out. In an instant, Joyce called the runner safe at first base which ruined the perfect game and no-hitter. It was clear the runner was out. Joyce got it wrong.

Not only did Joyce get it wrong. He blew the call. The television replay confirmed time after time that the runner was clearly out. It was clear the game should have been a perfect game.

It was also clear that Jim Joyce was overcome with emotion following the game after being confronted with the replay. He cried as he addressed the media following his personal apology to Galarraga. I watched his statement to the press as he said, "I just cost the kid a perfect game. I thought he beat the throw. It was the worst call of my career."

He blew it. He admitted it. That's refreshing.

We live in a world where the lines between right & wrong, true & false, and fact & fiction are often blurred. Truth is under attack in our world and it doesn't seem it will get better anytime soon. To admit we're wrong is considered a sign of weakness, frailty, and naivety. Jim Joyce faced his error in front of the world. It's not always easy for someone to admit that they were wrong especially when they caused hurt or pain to someone else.

Some will remember the game for the missed call which cost a young pitcher a perfect game. Some will remember the game for the controversy that followed the game. My hope is that some will remember because Jim Joyce admitted he was wrong.

It's especially remarkable to witness someone admit they were wrong following an execution. It's even more remarkable when that individual is supposed to be the picture of stoic strength. That's exactly what we find in Mark 15:39, "And when the centurion, who stood there in front of Jesus, heard his cry and saw how he died, he said, "Surely this man was the Son of God."

Centurions were strong. They commanded 100 men in the Roman army. They were the best of the best. They didn't make mistakes, and if they did, they didn't admit them or feel any sort of remorse.

Yet as Jesus cried out his last and breath escaped his body for the last time, the man responsible with overseeing his death acknowledged his true identity. After all of the torture, all of the mocking, all of the brutality, it was clear to this Roman centurion that Jesus was truly who he said he was. The same man that commanded the band of soldiers who gambled over Jesus' belongings and witnessed the suffering of the cross admitted he was wrong.

Have you ever been wrong about Jesus? It's not so uncommon. Many of us struggle from time to time with his identity. Some even set out to discover if he really was who he said he was.

C. S. Lewis was one of the greatest philosophers, writers, and defenders of Christianity in the last century. He was, however, not always that way. Lewis became an atheist as a teenager, determined that God could not exist in a rational world. I listened to a taped interview with Lewis once who described himself as an atheist being angry with God that he did not exist after he felt he had wasted so much time in church as a child.

Lewis' faith began to reemerge as an adult through the influence of his friend J. R. R. Tolkien and the writings of G. K. Chesterton. Lewis set out to prove to himself that Jesus could not have been divine. The end result was a lifetime of deep and abiding faith. Lewis used his position as a professor at the prestigious Oxford in England to write books and develop a platform for defending the faith in the twentieth century. He even developed a line of children's books set in the magical land of Narnia in order to tell the story of Jesus, sin, and redemption to children for decades to come. Lewis admitted that he was wrong about Jesus and spent a lifetime helping others to do the same.

I can't imagine the guilt the centurion must have felt.

After all, he crucified the Son of God.

He crucified an innocent man.

He drove the nails that held Jesus to the cross.

Or did he?

You see, Jesus wasn't held to the cross by nails or any other invention of man. Jesus was held to the cross by our sins. The centurion's viewpoint of Jesus on the cross isn't that much different than ours. It was my sin that held him there.

Sometimes I wonder what the centurion did with his discovery. What happened next? Early church history differs on what ever happened to the man. There seems to be very little evidence that his encounter with the identity of Jesus ever really impacted his life.

The Gospel writers routinely mentioned those by name in their narratives who would be recognized by the early church. Clearly the centurion's name is not given. Much like the rich young man in Mark 10, the man remains unnamed. Does that mean that he merely acknowledged Jesus for who he was but failed to yield his life to him? Did Mark not mention his name to protect him from his role in the violent and heinous death of Jesus? We'll never know. What we do know is that this man, for at least a moment, saw Jesus for who he was.

What do we do with that? Where does that lead us? You see it's not just enough for us to realize the identity of Jesus. It should inspire us. It should turn us upside down and inside out. Following Jesus can never be about our desire to simply know who he is. Following Jesus is about living for him because we know who he is.

14

Broken Barriers

"Some women were watching from a distance. Among them were Mary Magdalene, Mary the mother of James the younger and of Joses, and Salome . . . many other women who had come up with him to Jerusalem were also there."

—Mark 15:40–41

I LIKE talk radio. It drives my wife nuts. I have my favorite talk radio stations set as presets on my radio dial that I cruise back and forth between conversations. You know you like talk radio a bit too much when you start talking back to the host.

Not too long ago I found myself stuck in traffic on my way home from the office and I happened to hear a teaser for the next segment on a nationally syndicated talk radio program about an upcoming segment dealing with sexism and The Bible. I thought that sounded interesting enough and took my fingers off the presets. The host welcomed in a panel of experts interested in discussing what they perceived as several areas of sexism found within Scripture. They were particularly interested in the writings of Paul, the teachings of Jesus, and the Gospel narratives. Remember the part about talking back to the radio? I wanted to talk back very badly at that point.

The entire message of Jesus was about a revolution of breaking down barriers. Jesus broke down the barrier between God and

Man. He broke down the barriers of race when he visited with the woman at the well in Samaria. He broke down the barriers of maturity when he welcomed the children to his lap. And, Jesus broke down the gender barriers by allowing women to travel, participate, and support his ministry.

We don't think about that a whole lot. In fact, you almost miss it if you're not paying attention. We remember Peter, James, John, and even Judas. How often does anyone bring up the fact that it was the women who traveled with Jesus' ministry who helped support the ministry financially? How often does someone preach a sermon or write a book about the women involved in the day to day ministry performed by Jesus?

Mark ends his narrative in a way so contrary to the view of sexism that it would be impossible for anyone to confuse it. That is, of course, unless you've never read it. Mark is determined to mention the women and does so in three specific ways as his writing draws to a conclusion. You know why? Because Peter remembers the tremendous impact they had on the ministry of Jesus and the Holy Spirit is determined that impact be highlighted.

The first glimpse of the women comes at the crucifixion. Mark 15:40 says,

> "Some women were watching from a distance. Among them were Mary Magdalene, Mary the mother of James the younger and of Joses, and Salome. In Galilee these women had followed him and cared for his needs. Many other women who had come up with him to Jerusalem were also there."

It's interesting to note in the final moment of Jesus' life, it's not the eleven disciples (Judas was dead at this point) surrounding Golgotha and the cross. It's not the eleven disciples staying until the end. It's the women. It's not the rough and tumble fishermen. It's the mothers, housewives, and career women.

The women weren't there just to watch. They weren't there to speak when spoken to. They weren't there to herd the kids.

The women were there to attend to the needs of their Savior. The women were vital instruments in the ministry of Jesus.

The next mentioning of the women comes in the following passage when they accompanied Joseph of Arimathea to assist in removing the body of Jesus from the cross and conducting the burial. It was late in the day and the Sabbath was about to begin. They didn't have time to conduct all of the rituals of embalmment normally done for a Jewish burial. It was determined that the women would return on Sunday when the Sabbath expired.

It was when the women returned to the tomb in Mark 16 that the women made the greatest discovery in the history of the world. Mark 16 opens as the women were discussing the details of their trip. It was very early in the morning and they were preoccupied in trying to figure out who would roll the stone away from the entrance of the tomb. Mark 16:4–7 says:

> "But when they looked up, they saw that the stone, which was very large, had been rolled away. As they entered the tomb, they saw a young man dressed in a white robe sitting on the right side, and they were alarmed. "Don't be alarmed," he said. "You are looking for Jesus the Nazarene, who was crucified. He has risen! He is not here. See the place where they laid him."

It was important that the women had been a part of the initial burial process. They knew they were at the right tomb. They knew Jesus was dead on the slab in the tomb when they left. They knew he was no longer there.

It was not by chance that God revealed the resurrection to this group of faithful women. It communicated the ultimate message and confirmed the barriers broken down by the revolutionary message of Jesus. Women in First Century Palestine were literally second-class citizens. They had no right to own land, own businesses, or even vote. They were often shuffled around as property belonging to men. They never would have been allowed to have been a part of important discussions in the Synagogue.

With Jesus all of that changed. With Jesus there was no first or second-class. With Jesus there was no one of lesser importance or value. With Jesus, these women mattered. God chose to reveal the greatest moment and discovery of all of history to a group of women to show the importance of destroying barriers among the followers of Jesus.

The angel continued in verse 7, "But go, tell his disciples and Peter, 'He is going ahead of you into Galilee. There you will see him, just as he told you." Not only did God choose to reveal the resurrection to the women first, but he chose to make them his messengers as well. Women were not even allowed to testify in Jewish courts. Now, God was making these women the greatest witnesses of all time.

So much of the ministry of Jesus, so many of his encounters, his teachings, welcomed citizens of all tiers. No longer was religion about a blood-line, a birth order, race, or gender. True religion now was about a relationship with Jesus.

I couldn't help but think about this passage as I turned the radio off that day. If ever there was a place that welcomed both genders, all races, all ages, all backgrounds, all income levels, it is the Kingdom of God. He showed that to these faithful women so long ago. He continues to show that today. The Kingdom of God is not about where you come from, it's about where you're going on your journey with Jesus.

15

Peter and Us

IT'S EASY to give Peter a hard time. He's the hothead who cut off an ear. He's the loud mouth who always tasted his foot. He's the one whose faith always seemed to have a bigger bark than bite. He's the one who always seemed to speak first and think later.

I think I know Peter. He's a lot like me. Sometimes I struggle with the same things and in the same ways. Maybe we shouldn't be so quick to write him off.

When the angel gives instructions to the women at the tomb to share the resurrection, it's interesting to note that he separates the intended recipients. Mark 16:7 records the instruction, "But go, tell the disciples and Peter . . ." After all Peter had done? After everything he had said and done to deny Jesus in the very final hours of his life? Why Peter?

It seems like my lawn mower is the only one on the street not firing on all cylinders. It doesn't struggle the whole time. It runs great on my flat front yard. The struggles begin on the uphill climb on the side of the house. The mower huffs and puffs as it coughs its way up the hill while spewing enough white smoke to serve as an emergency SOS signal. The funny thing about it is that the little mower-that-could never seems to struggle in the flat areas or downhill slopes.

It made me think about my faith one night as I attempted to mow my yard. I'm pretty solid on the downhill slopes. I love those times of life. My faith seems to be a cinch when I'm rolling downhill.

It's when I turn uphill that things look a little different. If you're being honest, yours probably does the same. We don't always get going when the going gets tough. Our faith doesn't always elicit the stuff that inspires catchy motivational posters on the walls of the Christian bookstore down the street.

I used to look at the gospels and find a great sense of insecurity in my faith. After all, there was the tax collector who did a one-eighty. There were the friends determined to lower their afflicted friend through a hole in a roof to get to Jesus. There was the man who realized that Jesus was the only hope to save his daughter. There was the woman tired of living with her pain for more than a decade and knew if she could just get a touch from Jesus she would be healed. There was the man determined to carry the cross of Jesus and impact his family with his story.

On the other hand, there was the young man who simply couldn't alter the priorities of his life to follow Jesus. There were the teachers of the law upset that Jesus didn't do things their way. And if we're being honest, there were the disciples, scared every time the wind began to kick up. And there was Peter denying Jesus multiple times in one night after pledging a life of allegiance.

But Jesus wanted to see Peter immediately after his resurrection. Did you catch that? He actually wanted to see Peter. The same Peter who denied him multiple times. The same Peter who fled into the darkness to avoid being arrested with Jesus. The same Peter who sometimes struggled to grasp who Jesus really was after all that time. Jesus wanted to see Peter.

I used to pretend to be various superheroes when I was a child. If we're being honest, most of us live by the misconception that God desires us to be some sort of superheroes. We feel like he desires us to leap tall buildings of fear and fight the battles of life with one arm tied behind our back. The truth is that God never asks us to be superheroes. He's not nearly as concerned about our ability as he is our availability and Peter continually made himself available to God.

It's ok to cough, sputter, and struggle as long as we're allowing God to use us through those moments. If God required us to be well-oiled, leak-free, fine-tuned machines of faith, none of us would ever have a chance. Instead, He loves revealing his perfection through our imperfection. He loves showing his power through our moments of weakness. He loves us through the uphill climbs.

Maybe that's why there's a little bit of us in Peter. If we would have spent three years with Jesus, we would have struggled with the same concepts, asked the same questions, and had the same confusion. Peter shows us that it's ok to be on the journey, it's ok to be growing, it's ok to be a work in progress. It's not about our ability but our availability.

So, what do we do with Jesus? Maybe you've been a believer for a long time. Is that passion still the same? Maybe you've never quite wanted to give in to Jesus' calling on your life. Is there a better option? Maybe you're struggling in the direction Jesus is leading you right now. Have you given him the reigns?

What do we do with Jesus?

He's the same Jesus who shook the world during the First Century and continues to do so today. He's the same Jesus who moved and worked in lives then and still does so now. He's the same Jesus that restored relationships with God and still does so today. He's the same Jesus that broke down every barrier and calls us to do the same today.

What do we do with Jesus?

Peter followed him to his death.

Will we?

www.ingramcontent.com/pod-product-compliance
Lightning Source LLC
Chambersburg PA
CBHW060420090426
42734CB00011B/2385